"Laughter is the very essence of religion." - *Osho.*

LAUGHTER
The Best Meditation

Jokes to make you happy, healthy and holy

CW00762499

Compiled by
Inderjit Singh 'Jeet'

Editorial Direction by
Kul Bhushan

DIAMOND BOOKS

ISBN : 978-81-288-2533-0
© Author

Published by
DIAMOND POCKET BOOKS (P) LTD.
X-30, Okhla Industrial Area, Phase - II
New Delhi - 110 020
Phone : 011-41611861, 40712100
Fax : 011-41611866
E-mail : sales@dpb.in
Website : www.dpb.in

Edition : 2010

Printed at
Adarsh Printers, Delhi- 110032

Laughter – The Best Meditation
By: *Inderjit Singh 'Jeet'*

DEDICATION

In the sweet memory of my dear uncle,
Sohan Singh, the epitome of fun and frolic,
who stood by me through thick and thin,
and who taught me to laugh not only at myself,
but also at the vicissitudes of life.

- Inderjit Singh 'Jeet'

Introduction

Have We Forgotten to Laugh?

We have become so technically advanced that we have forgotten laughter. We have also forgotten to laugh at ourselves and at this crazy world we live in.

Osho, the enlightened master, gifted us a Laughter Meditation in his famous book, *Meditation: The Art of Ecstasy.* He says: "We are so attached to our suffering that laughing happens, generally, only as a release of tension. Only rarely, very rarely, does laughing happen without cause. We cannot laugh; we cannot be happy; even in our laughing there is pain. But laughing is so beautiful, such a deep cleansing, a deep purification."

Osho devised the Laughing Meditation. Practised every morning on awakening, it will be your day. Osho says, "If you wake up laughing, you will soon begin to feel how absurd life is. Nothing is serious: even your disappointments are laughable, even your pain is laughable, even you are laughable."

Here is the technique: when you wake up in the morning, before opening your eyes, stretch like a cat. Stretch every part of your body. Enjoy the stretching; enjoy the feeling of your body coming awake, alive. After three or four minutes of stretching, with your eyes still closed, laugh. For five minutes, just laugh. At first you will just be doing it, but soon, the sound of your attempt to laugh will cause genuine laughter. Lose yourself in laughter. It may take several days before you are really able to achieve this technique. We are not used to laughing; we have forgotten the easiest thing we could do. But keep trying; soon it will be spontaneous. And then, every morning, you wake up happy!

Another technique is to laugh by yourself when alone. This book, *Laughter: The Best Meditation* can help you to start your Laughter Meditation. When you read it and enjoy the jokes, laugh out aloud. At first, it will be difficult but you will soon get into the joy of laughter, so start with a soft "he-he-he". Then make it louder with a chuckle, a giggle, a snicker and finally with a full-throated guffaw as you roar with a full-belly laugh. Keep on for at least fifteen minutes. Then STOP suddenly and go into total silence. Now you will absorb all that energy deep inside you that was generated while laughing. Your mind will become completely silent, without any thoughts. This is when you are in meditation.

Osho says, "Let your laughter be your only prayer. Let your joy be your only offering. Love life! Love small things! Don't miss a single moment. Go on getting more and more joyful, and you will find God is coming to you more and more. My emphasis is to increase your cheerfulness, your laughter, because this world is not for the miserable. This world is not for the people who have become too accustomed to anxiety, anguish. This world belongs to those who live moment to moment in utter ecstasy. Cheerfulness, non-seriousness, a sense of humour to me, are very fundamental qualities of a religious being."

When asked, "What is your message?" Osho replied, "Be a joke unto yourself. Laugh at yourself. But learn to laugh. Seriousness is a sin, and it is a disease. Laughter has tremendous beauty, a lightness. It will bring lightness to you, and it will give you wings to fly."

- *Kul Bhushan*
kb@kulbhushan.net
www.kulbhushan.net

Foreword

Tickling the Funny Bone

Inderjit Singh 'Jeet' is a crusader fighting boredom in life. He knows that people are too much engrossed in their daily existence and have no time for a hearty laugh. In view of this, he wants people to spare some moments occasionally, to laugh over a book of jokes. As a result, they will find their burdens, cares and worries lightened. Life becomes enjoyable when one is capable of sharing jokes with others and, in the process, establishing a strong bond of bonhomie with them. Laughter is, in fact, a flash of light in the mind that dispels in a moment the darkness of misgivings and misapprehensions.

'Jeet', a well-known humorist, is the author of eight books in Punjabi on the art of wit and humour. He has been editing, for over a decade, a Punjabi journal *Meerzada*, presenting the sunny view of life artistically. The contributors to this journal make one tired of laughing off the blues. In this fast-changing world, humorous writing has a perennial place in the scheme of things. As such, jokes are bandied about from generation to generation without giving them time to get stale. One can say, jokes are for ever and are for ever new.

Indeed, jokes are double-faced like the Greek god Janus as they convey an apparent as well as a concealed meaning. The apparent meaning provokes laughter that acts as a balm to tense nerves. The concealed meaning reveals, in the process, the hidden treasure of thought-provoking gems. It is said that one who can laugh heartily can be relied upon, as his soul is bereft of the drowssiness of life. The book *Laughter: The Best Meditation* is surely a treasure trove for those who are eager to share jokes with others to make life a pleasant experience.

Prof. N. S. Tasneem
Former Fellow, Indian Institute
of Advanced Study, Shimla.

Preface

Jokes of All Shapes and Sizes
From A to Z

I always enjoyed jokes, especially risqué ones. My aim in compiling this book is all about making people laugh by taking chances and cracking jokes about those embarrassing incidents they don't like talking about. I make no claim to the yarns of this book; indeed I have heard most of them over the years from several sources: radio, television, newspapers, magazines and friends; and I have translated some of them from other languages like Hindi, Urdu and Punjabi. A few are adapted and recycled down the generations with only the names changed, not to defend the innocent, but to ensure we do not get sued by the guilty!

Jokes are known by the company they keep and their tendency to hit below the belt doesn't necessarily rule them out of order. Rude need not be crude, and some of the roughest ones can be salvaged with a different wording to retain the same punch line in an acceptable form.

Laughter: The Best Meditation is an engaging collection of jokes especially designed to refresh you and recharge you with meditation, and also dazzle your friends, disarm your enemies, impress your brothers and sisters and irritate those sitting on their high pedestals. You will find jokes of all shapes and sizes and on all topics – from A to Z.

Remember, there are numerous ways of laughing at jokes. You can laugh like a *hyena* or you can laugh your *head off* and *split your sides* at the same time. You can *laugh up your sleeve*, or from *the other side of your face*. You can even have *the last laugh*! But one thing is guaranteed. YOU WILL LAUGH.

I am grateful to Dr. Rajinder Singh for editing this compilation, Prof. N. S. Tasneem for his final approval before going to press and a well-known editor and author, Kul Bhushan, for his valuable suggestions, including the title, an introduction that gave a new direction to this book, and also for handling this project with the publishers who have done a splendid job.

- Inderjit Sigh 'Jeet'
13 Sharon Close
Wolverhampton
England WV4 6EU
Tel: 01902-659660
E-mail: jeetmeerzada@hotmail.co.uk

Profile

A Doctor of Humour With A Humour Store

Inderjit Singh 'Jeet' is a manufacturer and a wholesale trader in humour. He has already produced and distributed eight bags full of wit, much to the delight of his happy readers. As a matter of fact, he has a huge 'laughing stock' which he is bent upon clearing, and so he holds 'a cheering sale' every now and then. The sale price is very low for those in low spirits and very high for those in high spirits, in terms of time and not money!. Those in high spirits are afraid of sliding down in spirit and their time is valuable and time, being money for them, the cost is high for them.

Just look at him, he can't restrain himself from sharing. His latest product is *Laughter: The Best Meditation*. He is neither a mystic nor a spiritualist, and he is not a doctor in medicine either. In reality, he is a D. H. - a Doctor of Humour. For him, humour is the best medicine, humour is the best policy and humour is the best pastime for some, and a full time job for others like him. In his Humour Store, there are various sections at various levels. No one feels tired while going round all the sections, going up and down all the levels, as one section is better than the other and all the sections are better than any other section anywhere in any Store, whether it is 'Owlworth', 'Mares', 'Gracy', 'Martinet' or already defunct 'CamyClean'. By now, you must be itching to enter his store and go through the various sections and get boosted. Some of the Sections, as inscribed at the white board at the entrance alphabetically (one need not have the knowledge of alphabets) are: Animals, Advertisements, Ten Good Reasons Why Beer is Better Than Women? Blonds, Bumper Stickers, Children, Comic Dictionary,

Computers, Police, Doctors, Nurses, Men, Women, Politicians, Leaders, Lawmakers, Lawbreakers, Promise makers, Promise breakers, Husbands, Wives, Husbands Without Wives and Wives Without Husbands (with apologies to the great Hemingway).

'Why get stuck at the door of this store?' They are many sections, right from Nanny to Wannabe, as many as men thronging the place and elbowing others, men and women, pushing ahead or back, depending on who is ahead and who is at the back. Patience is all that is not required. There is more wit than wisdom but wit and wisdom are mixed up in such a way that it is not possible to have a *ratio-decidendi*. After all, 'Jeet' has brought out eight volumes of voluminous humour in his native tongue of that Five Rivers (since split into two and a half) but emotionally one. All his writings have a lasting effect as One Who Laughs, Lasts.

Born in 1934, 'Jeet' is a globetrotter, collecting herbs of humour, whether growing or about to grow in India, Kenya, England, United States, Canada, China and wherever you may go or may not go. Then he carries out grafting and drafting. He lived and worked in the Railways Headquarters (called a Board which is not blank) in India. Then he got married and carried away to Kenya where he made his home. But when the humour dried up, he migrated to England, the land of the Bard of Avon, and other outstanding humourous authors like Bernard Shaw, P. G. Wodehouse, Jerome K. Jerome, Evelyn Waugh and Douglas Adams, to name a few. They had more humour in them than they could contain, so they went on emptying their bags in books, in nooks, in Parliament and on stage. But Jeet's roots are in his native land and he delights in writing in his native tongue in which he wags, tags, rags, and mags, depending on his multifarious jovial temperament. For over a decade, he has single-handedly edited and published *Meerzada*, a quarterly magazine in Punjabi, noted for its humour and satire. In 2009, he was honoured as the *Punjabi Humour Writer of the Year*. May he live long till the world lasts and go on pinning hope for more!

- Dr Rajinder Singh.

Contents

Advertisements

Ads for Wives

Businessman: Wife wanted for company.

●

Farmer: Wanted: A wife from good stock; required for breeding.

●

Banker: Wanted: A wife who takes interest in me and credits me with the service.

●

Fisherman: Wife wanted: Must be able to dig, clean, cook worms and clean fish. Must have own boat with motor. Please send photographs of the motorboat.

●

Drunkard: Wanted: A girl. Girl's father should preferably have a drinks factory. Meet personally in a bar or send drinks for trial. Sample should be ample.

●

Car Dealer: Wanted: A sturdy, reliable, low depreciating wife. Should be in excellent working condition.

●

Builder: Wanted: A wife to help build on the foundations of my life. Must be homely and willing to build a relationship from the ground up.

●

Accountant: Searching for a figure with 5' 8" height, 36" width, 24" breadth. She should not make indulge in unnecessary expenses, but bring profit and credit to the family.

●

Mathematician: Wife required to complete the formula of my life. Must be numerate and understand complex algebra logarithms. Needed to help further my family unit.

●

Astronaut: I am searching for a wife to fill the space in my life; someone to share my universe. Must have looks that are out of the world.

●

Minicab Driver: Needed a wife to pick me up. Driving licence not necessary, but map-reading skills are a bonus.

●

Lawyer: I hereby propose to solicit myself as an eligible candidate for the post of husband after marriage. The person I'm looking for should be strictly a girl, with the evidence to support the view that she is a girl. The girl should be willing to surrender to the service of jurisdiction.

●

Advertisements

Advertising is the fine art of convincing people that debit is better than frustration.

●

Advertising tells us what unnecessary luxuries we can't do without.

●

Advertising is the fine art of making you think you have longed for something all your life that you have never heard of before.

●

Many small things have been made large by the right kind of advertising.

●

Advertising is the science of arresting human intelligence long enough to get money from it.

●

Half the money I spend on advertising is wasted, and the trouble is, I don't know which half.

●

Advertising helps to raise the standard of living by raising the standard of longing.

●

Advertising is like a marriage. There may be a better way, but what is it?

●

In good times, business people want to advertise. In bad times they have to.

●

To stop advertising to save money is like stopping your watch to save time.

●

If you think advertising doesn't work, consider the millions of British people who now think chicken curry tastes good.

●

Advertising sure brings quick results... last week I advertised for a night watchman; the same night my safe was robbed.

●

Advertising really changed our thinking. This morning my wife put on eye shadow, eye liner and eyelashes.

I said, "What are you doing to your eyes?"

She said, "I am making them look natural."

●

I have been in the advertising business for 20 years now. When I fill out a questionnaire and it says race... I put rat.

●

My kid returned from Sunday school with an illustrated card in his hand.

I said, "What have you got there?"

He said, "Uh, just an ad for heaven."

●

In the last couple of weeks I have seen ads for the Wonder Bra. Is that really a problem in this country – men not paying enough attention to women's breasts?

●

Girl wanted for petrol pump attendant.

●

Man wanted to wash dishes, and two waitresses.

●

Accommodation: Honeymoon suite, sleeps three.

●

Accommodation: Suits two girls willing to share room or young man.

●

Photographer setting up own business needs model, as sleeping partner or active partner.

●

Placed in the personal column: Fred please do not come home. All is forgiven.

●

Lost dog. Has three legs, blind in left eye, right ear missing, broken tail, no teeth, recently castrated. Answers to Lucky.

●

Used cars: Why go elsewhere to be cheated. Come here first.

●

Modular sofas: Only 199 dollars. For rest or foreplay.

●

One week sale of blankets: These bargain lots are rapidly shrinking.

●

Sheer stockings: Designed for fancy dress, but so serviceable that lots of women wear nothing else.

●

Our bikinis are exciting. They are simply the tops.

●

Toaster: A gift that every member of the family appreciates. Automatically   burns toast.

●

Four-poster bed; 101 years old. Perfect for antique lover.

●

Dog for sale: eats anything and is fond of children.

●

For sale: an antique desk suitable for lady with thick legs and large drawers.

Animals

A lion woke up one morning with the urge to inflict his superiority on his fellow beasts. So he strode over to a monkey and roared: "Who is the mightiest animal in the jungle?"

"You are master," said the monkey, quivering.

Then the lion came across a deer.

"Who is the mightiest animal in the jungle?" roared the lion.

"You are master," said the deer, shaking with fear.

Next the lion met an elephant.

"Who is the mightiest animal in the jungle?" roared the lion.

The elephant grabbed the lion with his trunk, slammed him against the tree half a dozen times dropped him like a stone and ambled off.

"All right," shouted the lion. "There's no need to turn nasty just because you don't know the answer."

●

A giant panda walked into a restaurant, He ordered some food, ate it, then pulled a gun and blew the brains out of the waiter. Alerted by the shots, the manager appeared just as the panda was making his way to the door.

"Hey, you!" yelled the manager. "You just shot my waiter. Where do you think you're going?"

The beast replied calmly: "I'm a panda. Look it up in the dictionary."

When the panda had gone, the manager thumbed the dictionary. Sure enough, under panda it said: "Furry animal, lives in China. Eats shoot and leaves."

●

Two lions were strolling down Broadway. One turned to the other and said:

"Not many people around today, are there?"

●

From where do you get virgin wool?
Ugly sheep.

●

Why did the homeless turtle cross the road?
To get to the Shell station.

●

What's black and white and goes round and round?
A zebra stuck in a revolving door.

●

How do you spot a modern spider?
He has a website.

●

What do you call an elephant that flies?
A jumbo jet.

●

How does an elephant get down from a tree?
He sits on a leaf and waits till autumn.

●

What do you get from a drunken chicken?
Scotch eggs.

●

What is the insect's favourite game?
Cricket.

●

How do you find where a flea has bitten you?
Start from the scratch.

●

What happened when the lion ate the comedian?
He felt funny.

●

What pillar doesn't need holding up?
A caterpillar.

●

What does the lion say to his friends before they go out hunting?
Let us prey.

●

How do you make a butterfly?
Flick it out of the butter dish with a knife.

●

Why was the glow-worm unhappy?
Because her children weren't that bright.

●

What did the lion say to his cubs when he taught them to hunt?
Don't go over the road till you see the zebra crossing.

●

Where do birds meet for coffee? In a nest-café.

●

What did the bee say to the naughty bee? Bee hive yourself.

●

What is the difference between fleas and dogs?
Dogs can have fleas but fleas can't have dogs.

●

What do you call a big fish that makes you an offer you can't refuse? The codfather.

●

What kind of tiles can't you stick on walls? Reptiles.

●

Why does a mosquito go to the dentist? To improve his bite.

●

Why is a sofa like a roast chicken?
Because they are both full of stuffing.

●

What is the definition of a caterpillar? A worm in a fur coat.

●

What do you call a cow with no legs? Ground beef.

●

What do you call a cow with two legs? Lean beef.

●

What do you call a deer with no eyes?
No eye idea.

Beer

Ten Good Reasons Why Beer is Better Than Women

1. You can enjoy a beer all month long.
2. Beer has no headache.
3. Beer is always wet.
4. You can share beer with your friends.
5. Beer does not demand equality.
6. You can have a beer in public.
7. Beer does not care when you come home.
8. A frigid beer is a good beer.
9. Beer does not get jealous when you grab another beer.
10. Beer is never late.

Blonde

I am not offended by all the dumb blonde jokes because I know I'm not dumb... and I also know that I'm not blonde. (Dolly Parton)

●

Why did the blonde climb the glass? To see what was on the other side.

●

How do you get a blonde to marry you? Tell her she is pregnant.

●

What do blondes and bottles have in common? Both are empty from the neck up.

●

A blonde went to the doctor. He examined her and said: "Stay out of bed for two days."

●

What do you do when a blonde throws a pin at you? Run like hell, she's got a grenade in her mouth.

●

Why did the blonde tiptoe past the medicine cabinet? She didn't want to awaken the sleeping pills.

●

Did you hear about the blonde who got an AM radio? It took her a month to realise she could play it in the afternoon.

●

What do you call a blonde with half a brain? Gifted.

●

Why did the blonde stare at the carton of orange juice? Because it said "concentrate".

●

Why did the blonde move to LA? It was easier to spell.

●

What's the difference between butter and a blonde? Butter is difficult to spread.

●

Why did the blonde climb to the roof? She heard that drinks were on the house.

●

Why did the blonde bury her driver's licence? Because it had expired.

●

What do you call a blonde with two brain cells? Pregnant.

Bumper Stickers

- Make love not war: See driver for details.
- Kids in the back seat cause accidents; accidents in the back seat cause kids.
- Trust in God, but lock your car.
- Marriage is not a word, it's a sentence.
- Good cowgirls keep their calves together.
- I bet you I could stop gambling.
- Caution! Driver applying make-up.
- Never mind the dog. Beware of the owner!
- Avoid hangovers. Stay drunk.
- Husbands are proof that women have a sense of humour.
- Niagara Falls and Viagra Rises.
- Don't drink and drive. If you hit a bump you spill your beer.
- Money is the route to all evils. Send £9.95 for more information.
- Horn broken, watch for finger.
- Lost your car? Look under my tyres.

- Flies spread disease. Keep yours closed.
- Madness takes its toll. Please have exact change.
- Atheism is a non-prophet organisation.
- Ssssh. The driver is sleeping.
- Ask not what you can do for me; just do it!
- Funny, I don't remember being absent-minded.
- All men are animals; some just make better pets.
- Born free…Taxed to death.
- Beauty is only skin deep. Ugly goes straight to the bone.
- Disney World: A people trap operated by a mouse.
- I got this motor for my wife; the best deal I ever made.
- Don't take my signals literally.
- A balanced diet is a cookie in each hand.
- Always remember you're unique, just like everyone else.
- Hug your kids at home and belt them in the car.
- Money is not everything, but it sure keeps the kids in touch.
- Forget about world peace; visualise using you turn signal.
- Give a man an inch and he thinks he's a ruler.
- Love may be blind, but marriage is a real eye-opener.
- Warning: I have an attitude and I know how to use it.
- Do Not Wash; this vehicle is undergoing a scientific dirt test.
- Ever stop to think, and forget to start again?
- Money can't buy love. But it can rent a very close imitation.
- This car is like my husband; if it is not yours don't touch it!
- Want to feel safe tonight? Sleep with a cop.
- Want a taste of religion? Bite a minister.
- I'd kill for a Nobel Peace Prize.
- I love animals, especially in gravy.
- To all you virgins: thanks for nothing.

Comic Dictionary

- **Adult:** Someone who was stopped growing at both ends and started growing in the middle.
- **Age:** A man is as old as he feels. A woman is as old as she looks.
- **Accountant:** A man hired to explain that you didn't make the money you did.
- **Advertising:** An advertising agency is 85 per cent confusion and 15 per cent commission.
- **Advice:** The only thing one can do with good advice is to pass on. It's never of any use to one.
- **Archaeologist:** Someone whose career is in ruins.
- **Alcohol:** A liquid good for preserving almost everything except secrets.
- **Alimony:** The cost of loving.
- **Americans:** People with more time-saving devices yet have less time than any one else in the world
- **Architect:** One who drafts a plan of your house, and plans a draft of your money.
- **Art:** Art is the most beautiful of all lies.
- **Autobiography:** A car's log book.
- **Baby:** A loud noise at one end and no sense of responsibility at the other.
- **Bachelor:** A man who prefers to ball without the chain.
- **Bacteria:** Back door to cafeteria.
- **Baldness:** When you have less hair to comb but more face to wash.

- **Banker:** A fellow who lends you his umbrella when the sun is shinning, but wants it back the minute it begins to rain.
- **Beauty-** The power by which a woman charms a lover and terrifies a husband.
- **Beauty-** Ugliness is, in a way, superior to beauty because it lasts.
- **Bigamy:** The maximum penalty for bigamy is two mothers-in-law.
- **Bookmaker:** A pickpocket who lets you use your own hands.
- **Bore:** A man who, when asked how he is, tells you.
- **Brain:** The apparatus with which we think that we think.
- **Bride:** A woman with a fine prospect of happiness behind her.
- **Budget:** A family's attempt to live below its yearnings.
- **Calendar:** Something that goes in one year and out the other.
- **Capitalism:** Survival of the fattest.
- **Chicago:** Virgin territory for whorehouses.
- **Chicken:** A creature you eat before it's born and after it's dead.
- **Children:** Creatures who disgrace you by exhibiting in public the examples you set for them at home.
- **Christian:** A man who feels repentance on a Sunday for what he did on Saturday and is going to do on Monday.
- **Christmas:** A holiday when neither the past nor the future is of as much interest as the present.
- **College Professor:** Someone who talks in other people's sleep.
- **Committee:** A group of the unwilling, chosen from the unfit, to do the unnecessary.
- **Computer:** Never trust a computer you can't throw out of the window.

- **Commuter:** A traveller who pays short visits to home and office.
- **Conference:** A gathering of important people who singly can do nothing, but together decide that nothing can be done.
- **Conservative:** A man with perfectly good legs who, however, has never learned how to walk forward.
- **Constipation:** To have and to hold.
- **Consultant:** Someone who takes the watch off your wrist and tells you the time.
- **Cosmetics:** A woman's means for keeping a man from reading between the lines.
- **Court of Law**: A place where a suit is pressed and a man may be taken to the cleaners.
- **Courtship:** The period during which the girl decides whether or not she can do any better.
- **Critic:** A man who knows the way but can't drive the car.
- **Cynic:** A man who knows the price of everything and the value of nothing.
- **Dentist:** One who, while putting metal into your mouth, pulls coins out of your pocket.
- **Diagnosis:** The physician's art of determining the condition of the patient's purse in order to find out how sick to make him.
- **Dictionary:** A place where success comes before work.
- **Diplomat**: A man who always remembers a woman's name, never her age.
- **Doctor:** Never trust a doctor who says you're dead. Get a second opinion.
- **Editor:** A fellow with a little desk and a big wastepaper basket.
- **Efficiency Expert:** Someone who is smart enough to tell you how to run a business but too smart to start his own.

- **Egotist:** Someone who is usually me-deep in conversation.
- **Epitaph:** A belated advertisement for a line of goods that has been permanently discontinued.
- **Experience:** The comb that nature gives us when we are bald.
- **Familiarity:** Familiarity breeds contempt – and children.
- **Fashion:** Brevity is the soul of lingerie.
- **Fisherman:** A jerk at one end of the line waiting for the jerk on the other end.
- **Flattery:** An insult in gift wrapping.
- **Freedom:** Man was born free, and everywhere he is in chains.
- **Friends:** Friendship is like money, easier made then kept.
- **Friendship:** A ship big enough to carry two in fair weather, but only one in foul.
- **Funeral Director:** A guy who tries to look sad during a 10,000-dollar funeral.
- **Gambling:** A sure way of getting nothing for something.
- **Genius:** A man who can do anything except making a living.
- **Grandparents:** People who think your children are wonderful even though they're sure you're not raising them right.
- **Gross Ignorance:** A hundred and forty-four times worse than ordinary ignorance.
- **Guests:** Fish and visitors smell after three days.
- **Hairdresser's:** A place where some women go to dye.
- **Handicap:** Ready-to-use cap.
- **Hanging:** A suspended sentence.
- **Handkerchief:** A small square of linen useful at funerals, to conceal a lack of tears. Also, a form of cold storage.
- **History:** A set of lies agreed upon.
- **Home:** Charity and beating begin at home.
- **Honesty:** Fear of being caught.

- **Honeymoon:** A vacation a man takes before starting work under a new boss.
- **Horse Sense:** Something a horse has, to prevent it from betting on men.
- **Humour:** A rich man's joke is always funny.
- **Husband:** A husband is what is left of the lover, after the nerve has been extracted.
- **Impotence:** Nature's way of saying, "No hard feelings".
- **Inflation:** What used to cost 20 dollars to buy now costs 40 dollars to repair.
- **Judge:** A law student who marks his own paper.
- **Justice:** A decision in you favour.
- **Language:** India and Pakistan are two countries separated by the same language.
- **Lawyer:** The only person in whom ignorance of law is not punished.
- **Liar:** A lawyer with a roving commission.
- **Literature:** A classic is something that everyone wants to have read and nobody wants to read.
- **Love:** Love's like measles; all the worse when it comes late in life.
- **Marriage:** A romance in which the hero dies in the first chapter.
- **Martyr:** One who sacrifices himself to the unavoidable.
- **Matrimony:** A knot tied by a preacher and untied by a lawyer.
- **Men:** Behind every successful man stand a proud wife and a surprised mother-in-law.
- **Middle Age:** When you are willing to get up and offer your seat to a lady, but can't.
- **Miser:** A person who lives poor so that he can die rich.
- **Mother-in-law:** A woman who destroys her son-in-law's peace of mind by giving him a piece of hers.

- **Music:** Classical music is the kind we keep thinking will turn into a tune.
- **Neighbour:** One who knows more about your affairs than you do.
- **Newspapers:** The most truthful part of a newspaper is the advertisements.
- **Opera:** Where a guy is stabbed in the back, and instead of bleeding, he sings.
- **Optimist:** A pregnant girl who rubs vanishing cream on her tummy.
- **Opportunist:** A person who starts bathing if he accidentally falls into a river.
- **Patriot:** A fellow who gets a parking ticket and rejoices that the system works.
- **Pessimist:** A person whose blood type is always B-negative.
- **Philosopher:** A person who confuses you sufficiently to make you believe he knows what he is talking about.
- **Poetry:** A form of ingenious nonsense.
- **Politician:** One who shakes your hand before elections and your confidence after.
- **Politics:** The art of preventing people from becoming involved in affairs which concern them.
- **Progress:** Is it a progress if a cannibal uses a knife and fork?
- **Prosperity:** A period when you spend money you don't have.
- **Psychiatrist:** Any man who goes to a psychiatrist should have his head examined.
- **Psychologist:** Someone whom you pay a lot of money to ask you questions your wife asks free of charge.
- **Quotations:** It is a good thing for an uneducated man to read quotations.
- **Raisin:** A worried-looking grape.

- **Regret:** Make the final payment on the engagement ring three months after the divorce is final.
- **Revenge:** An eye for an eye leads only to more blindness.
- **Sardines:** Little fish that crawl into a tin, lock themselves up, and leave the key outside.
- **Secret:** Something you tell one person at a time.
- **Sex:** No sex is better than bad sex.
- **Silence:** Silence is the virtue of fools.
- **Sleep:** Laugh and the world laughs with you; snore and you sleep alone.
- **Society:** There is only one thing in the world worse than being talked about, and that is not being talked about.
- **Stalemate:** A husband who has lost his ardour.
- **Striker:** Someone who is unsuited for work.
- **Success:** Success is a private affair. Failure is a private funeral.
- **Synonym:** A word you use when you can't spell the other.
- **Tact:** Tact is the ability to tell a man he's open-minded when he has a hole in his head.
- **Teacher:** He who can, does. He who cannot, teaches.
- **Television:** A device that permits people who haven't anything to do to watch people who can't do anything.
- **Theatre:** The aspirin of the middle classes.
- **Time:** Time wounds all heels.
- **Tomorrow:** One of the greatest labour saving devices of today.
- **Undertaker:** The last guy to let you down.
- **Vacuum Cleaner:** A broom with a stomach.
- **Vanity:** To love oneself is the beginning of a lifelong romance.
- **Vulgarity:** Other people's conduct.
- **Waiter:** One who thinks money grows on trays.
- **Warehouse:** What you ask when you are lost.

- ❑ **Wedding Ring:** The world's smallest handcuff.
- ❑ **Willy-nilly:** Impotent.
- ❑ **Wit:** A cultured insolence.
- ❑ **Women:** Women begin by resisting a man's advances and end by blocking his retreat.
- ❑ **Worry:** Interest paid on trouble before it falls.
- ❑ **Wrinkles:** Something other people have. You have character lines.
- ❑ **Writ:** Past tense of write.

Computers

You might be a computer nerd if:
- Your webpage is more popular than you.
- You refer to going to the bathroom as "downloading".
- When someone yells out, "Where's Tommy?" you do a search for tommy.com.
- You spend a plane trip with your laptop on your lap and your child in the overhead baggage compartment.
- You know exactly how much hard disc space you have free, but you don't know your wife's birthday.
- Your dog has its own home page.
- You name your daughter Dotcom.
- You run into your burning home to rescue your computer rather than your family.
- You e-mail your buddy who works at the desk next to you.
- You get into an elevator and double-click the button for the floor you want.
- Your optician looks deep into your eyes and sees a screen saver.
- You decided to stay on at college for an extra year just for the free Internet access.
- You read more books over the Internet than in your real life.

- Home is where you hang your @.
- You can't teach an old mouse new tricks.
- You check your mail: it says "no new message"; so you check it again.

Couples

"Yes, whatever time I get home, day or night, the wife always greets me with a kiss."

"Incredible! She really loves you."

"No. She just wants to find out if I've been drinking."

●

Husband: "This ointment makes my back smart."
Wife: "Would you like me to rub it on your head?"

●

Wife: "I've changed my mind."
Husband: "Thank heaven! Does it work better now?"

●

Newly wed husband: "I'll be very frank with you, dear, and tell you that you're not the first girl I've kissed."

Bride: "I'll also be frank, and tell you that you still have to learn a lot about kissing."

●

On their twentieth wedding anniversary a couple took a trip to the old country. While driving through the Black Forest, they came upon a sign that said, "Wishing Well – next left."

Though doubtful, the husband and wife took the next left turn and pulled over beside an old stone well. Getting out, the man read the instructions and, leaning over the well, threw in a penny and made a wish. Then his wife did likewise. However, when she leaned over she lost her balance, tumbled in and drowned.

Steeping back, the man cheered, "Hey! It really works!"

•

Waking up after a restless night, the wife turned to her husband and frowned, "I can't believe it! All night long, you kept cursing me in your sleep!"

The husband replied, "Who was sleeping?"

•

"Oh, God," sighed the wife one morning "I'm convinced my mind is almost completely gone!"

Her husband looked up from the newspaper and commented, "I'm not surprised: "You have given me a piece of it every day for twenty years."

•

Dr. Smith is walking out of the house after breakfast. He turns to his wife and barks, "You're a rotten wife, a crummy mother and a lousy lay!"

That night when he gets home he finds his wife on the living room floor with another man!

He yelps, "What do you think you're doing?"

She moans, "Getting a second opinion!"

•

The general's wife came home fuming from a party.

"What happened?" the general inquired, "Why are you in such a rage?"

"I met a nasty man at the party," the wife said. "He called me an old whore."

"Nothing to get peeved about, my dear....Why, I haven't been in the army for years, but people still call me general."

•

An old woman goes to the doctor and finds out, much to her surprise, that she is pregnant. She immediately calls her husband on the telephone, "You old stupid," she says. "You got me pregnant."

The husband pauses for a moment, and then asks, "Who is this?"

●

He: "You see, if enter into a companionate marriage we can live together for a while and then if we've made a mistake we can separate."

She: "Yes, but what'll we do with the mistake?"

●

An irate wife waited for her husband at the door. There was alcohol on his breath and lipstick on his collar.

"I assume," she snarled, "there's a very good reason for you to come waltzing in here at eight o'clock in the morning!"

"There is," he said. "Breakfast."

●

On their golden anniversary, a wife reminded her husband. "Do you remember when you proposed to me, I was so overwhelmed that I did not talk for an hour."

The husband replied, "Yes darling, that was the happiest hour of my life."

●

A man says to his wife on their wedding night. "Are you sure I am the first man, you have slept with?" She replies, "Of course, honey. I stayed awake with all others."

Courtship

A girl went over to her friend and said, "I hear you broke off your engagement to Rob. Why?"

"It's just that my feelings for him aren't the same any more."

"Are you returning his ring?"

"No way! My feelings for the ring haven't changed a bit."

●

A young couple parked in lover's lane. "It's lovely out here tonight," she sighed romantically. "It's so quiet and peaceful. Just listen to the crickets."

"They're not crickets," replied her boyfriend. "They're zippers.

●

He: "I'll kiss you on the chin!"

She: "Can't you raise your offer?"

●

"I just broke up with someone and the last thing she said to me was, 'You'll never find anyone like me again.'

I thought, "I should hope not! If I don't want you, why would I want someone like you?"

●

A girl phoned me the other day and said, "Come on over, there's no one at home."

I went over. No one was home.

●

He: "If you keep looking at me like that I'm going to kiss you."

She: "Well, hurry up. I can't hold this expression much longer."

●

A boy promised his girlfriend "We're going to have a great time on Saturday. I got three tickets for the big game."

"Why do we need three?" she asked.

"One for your father, one for your mother and one for your kid sister…."

●

I've been so many blind dates, I should get a free dog. (Wendy Liebman)

●

"What are the young man's intentions?"

"Well, he's been keeping me pretty much in the dark."

●

"My rose!" he whispered tenderly, as he pressed her velvet cheek to his.

"My cactus!" she said, as she dodged his whiskers.

●

"That young brother of yours saw me kiss you just now. What should I give him to keep quiet?"

"He usually gets £5," she said absent-mindedly.

●

He: "Tell me, darling, do you like my moustache?"

She: Between you and me, I don't."

●

"I shall love to share all your trials and troubles, Jack."

"But dear, I have none."

"No, not now, darling; I mean when we're married."

Doctors

When a pipe burst in a doctor's house, he was forced to call the plumber. The plumber came over, fiddled around for half an hour and presented the doctor with a bill of £200.

"£200 for half an hour's work! This is ridiculous! I don't make that much as a doctor!"

The plumber replied: "Neither did when I was a doctor."

●

An elderly patient to the doctor. "I need help, doctor. Do you remember those voices in my head which I've been complaining about for years?"

"Yes"

"Well, they have suddenly stopped."

"That's good. So what's problem?"

"I think I'm going deaf."

●

A woman went to the doctor and complained that she felt constantly exhausted.

"How often do you have sex?" asked the doctor.

"Every Monday, Wednesday and Friday," replied the woman.

"Well, perhaps you should cut out Wednesdays."

"I can't, that's the only night I'm home with my husband."

●

A man went to the doctor with a cucumber in his left ear, a carrot in his right ear and a banana up his nose. "What's wrong with me?" he asked.

"Simple," said the doctor. "You're not eating properly."

●

A woman went to the doctor. The doctor said, "You've got tuberculosis."

"I don't believe you," said the shocked woman. "I want a second opinion."

"All right," said the doctor. "You are ugly as well."

●

A woman went to the doctor clutching the side of her face.

"What seems to be the problem?" asked the doctor.

"Well", said the woman, removing her hand, "it's this pimple on my cheek. There's a small tree growing from it, and a table and chairs, and a picnic basket. What on earth can it be?"

"It's nothing to worry about," said the doctor. "It's only a beauty spot."

●

A man went to the doctor complaining of a pain in his stomach. The doctor gave him a thorough examination but could not find anything obviously wrong.

The doctor sighed: "I'm afraid I can't diagnose your complaint. I think it must be drink."

"All right then," said the patient, "I'll come back when you're sober."

●

A woman went to the doctor to ask what she could do to prevent getting pregnant.

He told her, "Drink tea."

"Before or after?" she asked.

"Instead," replied the doctor.

●

The National Health doctors staged a protest at Trafalgar Square, waving large placard. Unfortunately no one could read what they had written.

●

Four nurses decided to play a trick on a doctor whom they thought was arrogant. They discussed what each had done.

The first nurse said, "I stuffed cotton wool in his stethoscope so that he couldn't hear."

The second nurse said, "I let the mercury out of his thermometer and painted it to read 107 degrees."

The third nurse said, "I poked holes in all the condoms he keeps in his desk drawer."

And the fourth nurse fainted.

●

What is the difference between God and a doctor?
God does not think he is a doctor.

●

My doctor gave me six months to live but I couldn't pay the bill, so he gave me six months more.

●

A man went to the doctor because he had swallowed a bottle of sleeping pills.

The doctor told him to have a few drinks and get some rest.

●

Patient: "Doctor, doctor, I feel like a pack of cards."
Doctor: "I'll deal with you later."

●

Patient: "Doctor, doctor I keep thinking I'm a piece of chalk."
Doctor: "Get to the end of the cue."

●

Patient: "Doctor, doctor, I have a serious memory problem. I can't remember a thing."
Doctor: "How long have you had this problem?"
Patient: "What problem?"

●

Patient: "Doctor, doctor, people keep ignoring me."
Doctor: "Next!"

●

Patient: "Doctor, doctor, my son swallowed a razor."
Doctor: "Don't panic, I'm coming right away. Have you done anything yet?"
Patient: "Yeah, I shaved with an electric razor."

●

Patient: "Doctor, doctor, I think I'm a chicken."
Doctor: "How long has this been going on?"
Patient: "Ever since I was an egg."

●

Patient: "Doctor, doctor, I keep thinking I'm a bell."
Doctor: "If the feeling persists, give me a ring."

●

Patient: "Doctor, doctor, my hair keeps falling out. What can you give me to keep it in?"
Doctor: "A shoebox. Next."

●

Patient: "Doctor, doctor, what's good for excessive wind?"
Doctor: "A kite."

●

Nurse: "Doctor, there's an invisible man in the waiting room."
Doctor: "Tell him I can't see him."

●

Patient: "Doctor, doctor, people tell me I'm a wheelbarrow."
Doctor: "Don't let them push you around."

●

Patient: "Doctor, doctor, I have a split personality."
Doctor: "Nurse, bring in another chair."

●

Patient: "Doctor, doctor, I keep thinking I'm a clock."

Doctor: "All right, relax. There is no need to get yourself wound up."

●

Patient: "Doctor, doctor, I get so nervous and frightened during driving tests."

Doctor: "Don't worry, you'll pass eventually."

Patient: "But I'm the examiner."

●

Patient: "Doctor, doctor, I can't control my aggression."

Doctor: "How long have you had this problem?"

Patient: "Who wants to know?"

●

Patient: "Doctor, doctor, I've only 59 seconds to live."

Doctor: "Wait a minute please."

●

Patient: "Doctor, doctor, I think I'm a bridge."

Doctor: "What's come over you?"

Patient: "Two cars, a truck and a coach."

●

Husband: "So what should I pay you for curing my wife?"

Doctor: "Oh, pay me whatever you think she's worth to you."

And the husband immediately gave him five cents.

●

Mrs. Smith just gave birth to a child. She called the doctor of her ward and enquired if she could see her lawyer.

Doctor: "Why? Is something wrong with my hospital?"

Mrs. Smith: "Oh, no, it's not the hospital?" I want to divorce my husband.

Doctor: "Why do you want to divorce your husband? You have just given birth to a child. On what grounds do you want to divorce him?"

"Infidelity," Mrs Smith answered. "I don't think he's the father of my child."

●

"Are you sure?" An anxious patient asked his doctor. "Are you sure I'll recover? I've heard that doctors sometimes give wrong diagnoses and treat patients for pneumonia who later die of typhoid fever."

"That is sheer nonsense," replied the doctor. "If I treat a man for pneumonia, he dies of pneumonia."

●

After giving the patient a full medical examination the doctor explained his prescription as he wrote it out. "Take the green pill with a full glass of water after getting up. Take the red with a full glass of water after lunch and the blue pill with a full glass of water after dinner."

"What exactly is my problem, doctor?" asked the patient.

"You're not drinking enough water."

●

Three months passed but the old patient saw no improvement with the doctor's treatment. Finally, one day he said: "Well doctor, I'll go home tomorrow. I better die a natural death."

●

Then there's the drunk who was arrested for an illegal operation.

He opened a guy's head with, a beer bottle.

●

A college student was boasting that he had been to all the hospitals in town. Suddenly, one of the boys said "I don't believe that?"

"Why not?"

"Have you been to the Maternity Hospital?"

"Of course, I was born there."

●

Doctor: "Do you know the side effects of a birth control pill?"

Medical student: "Yes"

Doctor: "What's that?"

Medical Student: "Pregnancy."

●

Nervous Patient: "Doctor, I often feel like killing myself. What shall I do?"

Doctor: "Leave it to me."

●

Examiner: "Suppose, then, that you are the doctor in charge and the treatment I have just outlined has failed to restore the patient. What would you do?"

Medical Student: "I'd show him my bill."

●

Doctor: "Now tell me, what's wrong with you"?

Patient: "I'm worried about my future."

Doctor: "I'll give you a year's treatment. It'll be $100 a month."

Patient: "That takes care of your future! Now, what about mine?"

●

The doctor examining a little girl with his stethoscope said: "Big breaths."   'Yeah, and I am only twelve.'

●

A man says to the doctor, "Doc, my hearing's going. I can't even hear myself fart."

The doctor says, "Take these pills every day for a week."

The man says, "Will they make me hear better?"

The doctor says, "They'll make you fart louder."

●

Nurse: (to doctor): "Every time I lean over to take a Mr. Smith's heartbeat, it increases. Something's wrong."

Doctor: "Nothing's wrong. Just keep the top of your blouse buttoned."

●

A man suffering from a sore throat could hardly talk, so he went to a clinic after office hours. The doctor's pretty young wife opened the door.

"Is the doctor in?" he whispered.

"No," she whispered. "Come in."

●

A man goes to the doctor and tells him, "Doc, I am having a really hard time controlling my bladder."

The doctor replies, "Get off my new carpet! First!"

●

The old boozer had to see the doctor about his condition. "You know your problem is that you drink far too much. It'll be the death of you, I'm warning you!" said the doctor, and with that he pulled out a bottle from the man's pocket.

"What's this?" he exclaimed. "Why you even have the nerve to bring a bottle into my surgery!"

Quick as a flash the boozer said, "Oh, that, Sir…well, you see, Sir, I've just come from a holiday in India and that is…err…a bottle of the holy water."

The doctor pulled out the cork and took a sip of the contents. "Great heavens!"

He said, "This is gin."

"Glory be to God!" said the man, "Another miracle."

●

Patient: "Well doctor, how long do you think it will take me to recover from this accident?"

Doctor: "Do you mean physically or financially?"

●

The patient staggered up to the doctor, wincing. "Say, would you give me something for my head?"

Doctor looked up, "Why? What would I do with it?"

●

An elderly woman went into the doctor's office. When the doctor asked why she was there, she replied, "I'd like to have some birth control pills."

Taken aback, the doctor thought for a minute and then said, "Excuse me, Mrs. Smith, but you are 75 years old, what possible use could you have for birth control pills?" The woman answered, "They help me sleep better."

The doctor thought some more and asked, "How in the world do birth control pills help you to sleep?"

The woman said, "I put them in my granddaughter's orange juice and I sleep better at night."

●

A man goes to the ophthalmologist. The receptionist asks him why he is there. The man complains "I keep seeing spots in front of my eyes."

The receptionist asks, "Have you seen the doctor?" And the man replies, "No just spots."

●

A woman went to a new doctor for a check-up. The doctor told her he was going to put his hand to her back and he wanted her to say eighty-eight.

"Eighty-Eight" she purred.

"Good. Now I am going to put my hand on your throat and I want to you to again say eighty-eight."

"Eighty….eighhhttt."

"Fine. Now I am going to put my hand on your chest and I want you once more to say eight-eight.

"One, two, three, four, five…."

●

"Doctor, Doctor, I think I need glasses."
"Yes, you certainly do, Sir, this is Fish and Chips shop."

●

Patient: "Doctor, Doctor, I feel like a £10 note."
Doctor: "Well go and buy something, then, the change will do you good."

●

Doctor: "I will examine you for twenty dollars."
Patient: "Go ahead, Doctor. If you find them you can have them."

●

Patient: "Doctor, I have a small, embarrassing wart."
Doctor: "Divorce him."

●

A man went to the doctor to be examined.
He said: "I keep losing my temper."
Doctor: "I beg your pardon."
He snapped: "I told you once, you fool.....!"

●

A woman went to see her doctor and explained that she was worried about getting pregnant.
"But," said the doctor, I put you on the pill."
"Yes I know," replied the woman. "But it keeps falling."

●

A lady who had borne eight children went to her doctor to ask him for a hearing aid, saying she really did not want to have any more children.
"You need contraceptive advice, not a hearing aid," said the doctor.
"No doctor, I want a hearing aid. Every Friday night when my husband comes back drunk from the pub, he gets into bed and says, "Do you want to go to sleep or what?" I am a bit deaf, and I always say, "What?"

●

A pretty young girl went to her doctor with a throat infection. As he was on holiday, she saw the replacement, who asked her to say "Ah!"

"That makes a change," she said, "most men only ask me to say yes!"

Drinking

The drunk gave the constable who was holding him up a hazy look, and asked, "What am I here for?"

"Drinking," said the sergeant at the desk.

"Oh good! I'll have a double whisky with soda."

●

Drunk: "Call me a taxi."

Barman: "Certainly Sir. You are a taxi."

●

A drunk slowly staggered through the park and came across a man doing push-ups. He watched for a minute then mumbled. "Excuse me old boy, but she's gone."

●

A drunk asked a woman the way to Alcoholics Anonymous.

"Do you wish to join?" Inquired the woman.

"No," was the reply, "to resign."

●

Mary: "What's your favourite drink?"

Sue: "The next one."

●

"If your wife is so beautiful, why do you get drunk every night?" Asked the first drunk.

"So I can see two of her," replied the second drunk.

●

Man: "Do you serve women in this bar?"
Barman: "No, you have to bring your own."

●

The social worker knocked on the door which was opened by a woman.

"Good evening. I am collecting for a home for drunkards?" Said the caller.

"Would you care to make a donation?"

"I certainly would," replied the woman. "Come back after the pubs shut and I'll give you my husband."

●

"I left a bottle of whisky in the train this morning."

"Was it turned into the lost and found department?"

"No, but the man who found it was."

●

Inspector: "What made you think the man was drunk?"
Constable: "He was having a heated argument with a taxi driver."
Inspector: "But that doesn't prove anything."
Constable: "Well Sir, there was no taxi driver."

●

The intoxicated diner beckoned the waiter over to his table.

"Waiter, I feel I have had too much to drink. Will you please bring me something to sober me up quickly?"

"Certainly, Sir, I'll get your bill."

●

Alcohol is good for you. My grandfather proved it. He drank two quarts of booze every mature day of his life and lived to the age of a hundred and three. I was at his cremation and that fire would not go out.

●

A drunk on a bus was tearing a newspaper into small pieces and throwing them out of the window.

"Excuse me," said a man sitting next to him. "Why are you tearing the paper and throwing the pieces out of the window?"

"To scare away the elephants," said the drunk.

"I don't see any elephants," said the man.

"Effective, isn't it?" Smiled the drunk.

●

Doctor: "Do you realise that every drink you take shortens your life by a month?"

Patient: "That can't be right, doctor, otherwise I would have been dead for the last twenty years."

●

A man walked into an English pub and ordered eighteen pints of beer.

"Have you a party outside?" asked the barman.

"No, they're for me."

"Eighteen pints?" questioned the barman.

"Well, it's your ruling," said the Irishman pointing to a sign over the bar: "No one is served under eighteen."

●

The painter fell off the ladder which was lying on the pavement. The foreman rushed up and shouted, "This man has just fallen ten feet. Give him a glass of water."

The painter eased himself up on one elbow and asked, "How far do I have to fall to get a glass of whisky?"

●

When Dean Martin was told that whisky killed more people than bullets, the star replied, "That may be true, but I'd rather be full of whisky than full of bullets."

●

The Irishman wanted to return to Ireland but was £1 short of his fare. He walked into a London pub and asked in a loud voice, "Has any one here got £1 to send a poor homesick Irishman back to the land of his fathers?"

"Certainly," said a happy drunk sitting at the bar.

"Here's £20, Take another nineteen with you."

●

"Sorry I am late dear, but I was competing in a beer-drinking contest at the pub," said the happy husband.

"Oh, really," said his wife coldly. "And who came second?"

●

Two terrorists had a few drinks together before setting out on a bombing mission. They got into the car and the passenger placed a bomb on his lap.

"I better not drive too fast," said the driver, "or the bomb you're carrying might go off."

"Doesn't matter," slurred the passenger, "Go as fast as you like, there's another in the boot."

●

I am bringing my son up to be like me. His schoolteacher asked him the meaning of the word "straight" and he answered, "Without soda."

●

First Drunk: "Do you know what time it is?"
Second Drunk: "Yes."
First Drunk: "Thanks."

●

One should never drink on an empty stomach.
Be wise. Have a couple of beers first.

●

Denis: "Drink makes you look very beautiful and sexy."
Margaret: "But I haven't been drinking."
Denis: "No, but I have."

●

A drunk staggered up to the owner of a pub and shook a finger at him.

"I want to complain about your barman in the lounge upstairs," panted the drunk.

"What happened?" asked the owner.

"He kicked my hat down the stairs, that's what he did."

"Probably having a little joke, surely you don't mind that?" coaxed the owner.

"Well, I do mind," insisted the drunk, "I was wearing the hat at the time."

●

A policeman observed a man sitting in a lay-by throwing empty beer cans out of the car window.

"What do you think you're doing?" asked the policeman.

"I am on the works outing."

"But you're alone."

"I know," said the man. "I am self-employed."

●

Patient: "Doctor, I keep thinking I'm a bottle of gin."

Doctor: "What you need is a little tonic."

●

The two drunks met at the bar.

"What's the date today, Sammy?" asked one.

"Don't know," replied Sammy.

"Well, look at the newspaper in your pocket."

"No use," said Sammy, "It's yesterday's."

●

Three drunks stagger into a pub near closing time. One collapses in a heap on the floor. The others order a brandy each.

"What about him?" asked the barman indicating the bundle on the floor.

"No more for him," replied one of the drunks, "he is driving."

●

The husband staggered into his house and \
by his angry wife.

"Drunk again!" she exclaimed. "I see you walk
and had the good sense not to drive."

"Couldn't get the car started."

"What's the matter with it?"

"There's water in the carburettor."

"Where is the car?"

"In the river."

●

The patient held out his hands and said, "Look, doctor,
. my hands won't stop shaking."

Looking at the hands the doctor asked, "Do you drink
much?"

"No, replied the patient, "I spill most of it."

●

He was too drunk to drive, so one of his friends put him in
a taxi. When they arrived at the street the driver was told to
go to, he asked "What's the number of your house?"

"Don't ask silly questions," said the drunk, "it's on the door."

●

She: "I have no sympathy for a man who gets drunk
every night."

He: "A man who gets drunk every night doesn't need
sympathy."

●

Don't drink and drive: It spills all over the steering wheel.

●

Two men sat in a pub knocking back beer after beer.

"You know, David, I think I'll buy this pub."

"Wait till we've had a few more drinks," said David, "and
I'll sell it to you."

●

"I think you've had enough Sir," said the barman.

"Nothing of the sort."

"Sir, you are blind drunk."

"Let me tell you, I am not blind drunk, I can see very well. Look, there's a one-eyed cat coming into the bar."

"Sir, that cat has two eyes and it's going out."

●

She: "I know everything. A policeman picked you up at three in the morning when you were embracing a lamppost."

He: "My dear, surely you're not jealous of a lamppost."

●

A lady walks into a bar that has a sign: "For Men only."

"I am sorry ma'am," says the bartender. "We only serve men in this place."

"That's fine," she says, "I'll take two of them."

●

The car sped down the highway, went through the guardrail, rolled down a cliff, bounced off a tree and finally shuddered to stop. A passing motorist who witnessed the entire accident, helped the miraculously unharmed driver out of the wreck.

"Good lord, mister," he gasped. "Are you drunk?"

"Of course" said the man, brushing the dirt from his suit. "What the hell do you think I am? A stunt driver?"

●

Beauty is in the eye of the beer holder.....

●

One day an Englishman, a Scotsman and an Irishman walked together into a pub. They each bought a pint of Guinness. Just as they were about to enjoy their creamy beverage, three flies landed in each of their pints, and got stuck in the thick foamy head. The Englishman pushed his bear away with disgust. The Scotsman fished the fly out of his bear and continued drinking, as if nothing has happened. The

Irishman, too, picked the fly out of his drink, held it out over the beer and shouted angrily, "SPIT IT OUT, SPIT IT OUT, SPIT IT OUT!!!"

●

Scientists in the United States revealed that beer contains small traces of female hormones.

To prove their theory, they fed one hundred men twelve pints of beer and observed that 100 per cent start talking nonsense and couldn't drive.

●

Jock was travelling by train and was seated next to a stern-faced clergyman. As Jock pulled out a bottle of whisky from his pocket, the clergyman glared and said reprovingly, "Look here, I am 65 and I have never tasted whisky in my life."

"Don't worry, Minister," smiled Jock, pouring himself a dram, "There is no risk to your starting now."

●

A man walks into a bar and asks for a beer. After drinking it, he looks into his shirt pocket and asks for another beer.

After drinking that, he looks into his shirt pocket again and asks for a third beer. This happens several times before the curious bartender asks him, "Every time you order a beer, you look into your shirt pocket. Why?"

The man replies, "I have a picture of my wife in there, and when she starts to look good, I'll go home."

●

A drunk was driving through the city and his car was weaving across the road. Eventually a cop pulled him over.

"Did you know," said the cop "that a few intersections earlier, your wife fell out of your car?"

"Oh, thank heaven," sighed the drunk. "For a minute, I thought I'd gone deaf."

●

They're trying to put warning labels on liquor bottles saying: Caution, alcohol can be dangerous for pregnant women.

That's ironic. If it weren't for alcohol, most women wouldn't even be that way.

Excuses

A traffic cop pulled over a guy who was driving erratically. "Blow into this breathalyser tube please," he ordered.

"Sorry officer, I can't. I am haemophiliac. If I do that, I'll bleed to death."

"Well then we'll need a urine sample."

"Sorry officer, I can't. I am diabetic. If I do that, I'll get really low blood sugar."

"All right. Then I need you to step out of your car and walk along this white line."

"Sorry officer. I can't."

"Why not?"

"Because I am drunk."

●

"Do you believe in life after death?" the company boss asked one of his young employees.

"Yes Sir."

"That's good, because after you left early yesterday to go to your grandmother's funeral, she called in to see you."

●

The driver was speeding down the highway late in the afternoon when he saw a police car behind. For a while he tried to out race his pursuer, but, after touching 120 and still not managing to shake him off, he realised it was a lost cause and pulled over.

The cop stepped out his car. "Listen, bud," said. "I've had a really lousy day and all I want t get home to my wife and kids. So if you can come up good excuse as to why you were doing 120 back ther let you off."

The driver thought for a moment and said, "Three weeks ago, my wife ran off with a cop. When I saw you in my rear-view mirror, I thought you were that officer and that you were trying to hand her back."

●

A woman saw an electrician walking up her drive. She rushed to the door. "Why have you come today?" she barked. "You were supposed to repair the doorbell yesterday."

"Yes, I know," said the electrician. "I rang three times but there was no answer."

●

For the Military

Captain: "Why did you volunteer for the undercover?"

Soldier: "I thought it meant I'd be working in bed."

●

General: "Why were you running away from the battle?"

Soldier: "I was practising for retreat."

●

Sergeant: "What were you before you were in the army?"

Soldier: "Much happier."

●

Sergeant: "Soldier, your bunk is a disgrace."
Soldier: "I know, but it's the only one you gave me."

●

Sergeant: "Why did you run for cover when that star passed by?"
Soldier: "They said it was a shooting star."

●

Sergeant: "Why didn't you clean up your footlocker?"
Private: "You said it was time for mess."

●

Sergeant: "Why has it taken you all morning to dig a foxhole?"
Soldier: "I couldn't find a fox."

●

General: "Why didn't you go to target practice?"
Soldier: "I was afraid you'd make me the target."

●

General: "Why didn't you follow the order to charge?"
Private: "I don't have a credit card."

For Shops and Shopping

Bank customer: "Why did you hit me on the head with that bag of change?"

Tiller: You said you wanted your money in a lump sum."

●

Box officer clerk: "Young man, I can't sell you a ticket. You should be in school now."
Young customer: "No, it's all right. I have measles."

●

Clerk: "That suit looks nice. It fits like a bandage."
Customer: "Thanks, I bought it by accident."

●

Clerk: "Would you like to buy a pocket calculator?"
Customer: "No, thanks. I know how many pockets I have."

●

Customer: "Couldn't you see I was going bald?"
Barber: "No, the shine from your bald head blinded me."

●

Customer: "I'd like a watch that tells the time."
Clerk: "Don't you have a watch that tells the time?"
Customer: "No, you have to look at it."

Food

At the food festival a man told the audience that there was one food item that was most dangerous to eat.

"And we all have to eat it, or will eat it." He said. "Can anyone here tell me which food causes the most grief and suffering for years after eating it," he asked.

A 75-year-old man in the front row stood up and said, "Wedding cake."

●

The Sunday school teacher asked, "Now Johnny, tell me frankly do you say your prayers before eating?"

"No Sir," Johnny replied "I don't have to, my mom is a good cook."

●

The children were lined up for lunch in a cafeteria of a Catholic elementary school. At the head of the table was a large pile of apples. The nun made a note and posted it on the apple tray. "Take one. God is watching."

Moving further along the lunch line, at the other end of the table was a large pile of chocolate chip cookies. One child whispered to another, "Take all you want. God is watching the apples."

●

A friend and I were standing in line at a fast food restaurant, waiting to place our order. There was a big sign that read: No bill larger than $20 will be accepted. The woman in front of us, pointing to the sign remarked, "Believe me, if I had a bill larger than $20 I wouldn't be eating here."

●

It was mealtime on a small plane and the stewardess asked a passenger if he would like dinner.

"What are my choices?" he asked.

She replied, "Yes or No."

●

Two students were talking about cooking. "I got a cookbook a couple of years ago," said one, "but I could never do anything with it."

"Was it too demanding?" asked his friend.

"Absolutely." Every one of the recipes began the same way: "Take a clean dish."

●

Two tomatoes were crossing the street, one in front of the other. The first tomato was getting impatient because the second one was so slow. Then halfway across, the second tomato was run over by a car. The first tomato shouted:

"Hey, ketchup."

●

Boy: "Are caterpillars good to eat?"

Father: "I have told you before: don't talk about such things at the dinner table."

Mother: "Anyway, why do you ask?"

Boy: "Because I saw one on Daddy's lettuce, and now it's gone."

●

I'm not saying my wife is a terrible cook, but our garbage has developed an ulcer. (Henry Youngman)

●

Scientists have discovered a food that diminishes a woman's sex drive by 90 per cent: the wedding cake!

●

Why did the tomato blush?
Because it saw the salad dressing.

●

What is Snow White's favourite drink?
Seven up.

●

What can you make from baked beans and onions?
Tear gas.

●

What is a Honeymoon Salad? Lettuce alone, with no dressing.

●

I am on my seafood diet right now!
How does it work?
Whenever I see food I eat it.

●

What do you get when you put three ducks in a box? A box of quackers.

●

I trained my dog not to beg at the table.
How did you do that?
I let him taste my cooking.

●

What do cats call mice on skateboards? Meals on Wheels.

●

Why did they let the chicken join the band? Because he had the drumsticks.

●

Why did the potato cross the road? He saw a fork up ahead.

●

Why did the raisin go out with the prune? Because he couldn't find a date.

●

What's smelly, round and laughs? A tickled onion.

●

Why did the baby strawberry cry? Because his mother was in a jam.

●

How do you repair a broken tomato? Tomato Paste.

●

Waiter, waiter! What is this bug doing in my salad? Trying to find its way out Sir!

●

Waiter, waiter! There is a caterpillar in my salad. Don't worry, there is no extra charge.

●

What kind of lettuce did they serve on the Titanic? Iceberg.

●

How can you tell if an apple is organic? Look for a healthy worm.

Sign in a restaurant window: Eat now; Pay waiter.

●

Eat, drink and re-marry, for tomorrow we diet.

●

Wife: "The two things I cook best are meatloaf and apple pie."Husband: "Which is this?"

Grandparents

The young boys were spending the night at their grandparents'. At bedtime, the two boys knelt beside their beds to say their prayers when the youngest one  began praying at the top of his lungs, "I pray for a new motorcycle; I pray for a new VCR."

His elder brother leaned over, nudged him and said, "Why are you shouting your prayers? God isn't deaf."

To which the little brother replied, "Bo, but grandpa is!"

●

A grandmother was giving directions to her grandson, who was coming to visit her with his wife.

"Come to the front door of the apartment complex. There is a panel at the door. With the elbow, push the button for 14 D. I will buzz you in. Come inside and with your elbow hit the door bell."

"Grandma, that sounds easy, but why am I hitting all the buttons with my elbow?"

"Are you coming empty handed?"

●

A grandfather and grandmother were sitting and talking when their young granddaughter asked, "Did God make you?"

"Yes, God made me," the grandfather answered.

"Did God make me too?"

"Yes, he did." The old man answered.

For a few minutes, the little girl seemed to be studying her grandpa, as well as her own reflections in the mirror, while her grandfather wondered what was running through her mind.

At last she spoke up.

"You know Grandpa", she said. "God's doing a much better job lately."

●

My grandmother moved in with our family of five. As I was brushing my teeth one morning, she tapped on the door.

"Is anyone there?"

I mumbled an answer, to which she replied, "Is that a yes or a no?"

●

A boy visited his grandmother with his friends. While the boy was talking to his granny in the kitchen, his friend was eating peanuts from the bowl on the living room table. When it was time to go, the friend called out: "Thanks for the peanuts."

"You're welcome," said granny. "Since I lost my dentures I can only suck the chocolate off them."

●

"I got this great new hearing aid the other day," said the granddad to his grandson.

"Really? Are you wearing it now?" asked the grandson.

"Yup," came the reply. "Cost me four thousand dollars.

"What kind is it?"

"Twelve-thirty."

●

My grandson was visiting me one day when he asked, "Grandma, do you know how you and God are alike?" I was mentally polishing my halo while I asked, "No, how are we alike?"

"You both are old," he replied.

●

What Are Grandparents?

1. Grandparents are a lady and a man who have no little children of their own. They like other people.
2. They can take their teeth and gums out.
3. Usually grandmothers are fat, but no too fat to tie your shoes.
4. Everyone should try to have grandparents, especially if you don't have them.

Health

Jack died. His lawyer stood before the family and read out Jack's last will and testament:

"To my dear wife Esther, I leave the house, 50 acres of land and one million

dollars. To my son Barry, I leave the big Lexus and the Jaguar. To my daughter Suzy, I leave my yacht and 25,000 dollars. And to my brother-in-law, Jeff, who always insisted that health is better than wealth, I leave my treadmill."

●

When a physician remarked on a new patient's "extraordinary ruddy complexion" he said, "High blood pressure Doc. It came from my family."

"Your mother's side or your father's side?" he asked.

"Neither," he replied. "It's from my wife's family."

"How could your wife's family give you blood pressure?" The doctor asked.

The patient sighed, "You ought to meet them sometimes, Doc."

●

A blonde was overweight, so her doctor put her on a diet.

"I want you to eat regularly for two days, then skip a day and repeat the procedure for two weeks. The next time I see you, you'll have lost five pounds."

When the blond returned, she had lost nearly 20 pounds.

"Why, that is amazing." The doctor said, "Did you following my instructions?"

The blonde nodded, "I will tell you, though, I thought I was going to drop dead that third day."

"From hunger you mean?" said the doctor.

"No, from skipping," replied the blond.

●

A woman went with her husband for his routine check-up. Later, the doctor took her to one side and said, "I'm afraid I have some bad news. Unless you adhere to a strict routine, your husband will die. Every morning, you must give him a good healthy breakfast and you must cook him a nutritious meal at night. Furthermore, you must not burden him with household chores and you must keep the house spotless and germ-free. I know it places a great deal of work on your shoulders, but it really is the only way to keep him alive."

On their way home, the husband asked his wife what the doctor had said to her. "Oh," she replied, "he said you're going to die."

●

A man went into a drugstore and asked the pharmacist if he could give him something for hiccups. Without warning, the pharmacist suddenly reached out and slapped the man hard across the face.

"What did you do that for?" he asked.

"Well, you haven't got hiccups any more, have you?"

"I haven't got hiccups; my wife has!"

●

Suffering from a bad case of the flu, the outraged patient bellowed "Three weeks? The doctor can't see me for three weeks? I could well be dead by then."

Calmly the voice at the end of the line replied, "If so, would you please have your wife call to cancel the appointment."

●

An overweight blond consulted her doctor for advice. The doctor advised that she run ten miles a day for thirty days. This, he promised, would help her lose as much as 20 pounds.

The blond followed the doctor's advice and after thirty days she was pleased to find that she had indeed lost nearly twenty pounds. She phoned the doctor and thanked him for the wonderful advice which produced such effective results.

At the end of the conversation however, she asked one last question.

"How do I get home, since I am now 300 miles away?"

●

A man had just arrived home after the successful implantation of a pacemaker.

Reading through the literature, he was delighted to learn that the instrument carried a lifetime guarantee.

●

Q. "Will the National Health Service be any different in the next century?"

A. "No. But if you call right now, you might get an appointment by then."

●

First man: "I tried to kill myself yesterday by taking 1,000 aspirin."

Second man: "What happened?"

First man: "Oh, after the first two I felt better."

●

After receiving his medication from the pharmacist, the customer inquired: "Are these time-release pills?"

"Yes," said the pharmacist. "They begin to work after your cheque is cleared."

●

It was the healthiest town in the region. They had to shoot a bloke to start a cemetery.

The only bloke to die over the last ten years was the undertaker. And he died of starvation.

●

Health is what my friends are always drinking to before they fall down.

●

Imagination

Several weeks after a young man had been hired, he was called into the personnel manager's office.

What is the meaning of this?" The manager asked. "When you applied for the job, you told us you had five' years' experience. Now we discover this is the first job you've ever had."

"Well," the young man said, "in your ad you said you wanted someone with imagination."

●

The attractive teacher tells the school children that today they have to use their imagination.

She says, "I have something red and round behind my back. What is it?"

Mary answers, "Is it an apple, Miss?" "No Mary. It's a cricket ball but it shows you were using your imagination."

She goes around the class with questions like this and then she tells the children to make her use her imagination.

Johnny raises his hand and says, "Miss, I have something that is one inch long and has a one centimetre knob on it. What is it?"

The shocked teacher says, "Johnny, you rude little......!"

"No, Miss," replied Johnny, "It's a matchstick, but it shows you are using your imagination."

●

Interviewer: "Just imagine you are on the third floor and it caught fire. How will you escape?"

Job Applicant: "It's simple. I will stop my imagination!"

●

The basis of action is lack of imagination. It is the last resource of those who know not how to dream. *(Oscar Wilde)*

●

The genius of Man in our time has gone into jet-propulsion, atom-splitting, penicillin-curing, etc. There is none over for works of imagination; of spiritual insight or mystical enlightenment. I asked for bread and was given a tranquiliser."

(Malcolm Muggeridge)

●

Imagination was given to man to compensate him for what he is not; a sense of humour to console him for what he is."

(Francis Bacon)

●

When I was a kid, I used to imagine animals running under my bed. I told my dad, and he solved the problem quickly. He cut the legs off the bed."

(Lou Brock)

●

Imagination! Imagination! I put it first years ago, when I was asked what qualities I thought necessary for success upon the stage." *(Ellen Terry)*

●

Belief in the supernatural reflects a failure of the imagination." *(Edward Abbey)*

Jobs

Deer Sir,

I waunt to apply for the secritary job what I saw in the paper. I can Type real quik wit one finggar and do sum a counting.

I think I am good on the phone and no I am a pepole person, Pepole really seam to respond to me well.

Im lookin for a Jobb as a secritary but it musent be to complicaited.

I no my spelling is not to good but find that I Offen can get a job thru my persinalety. My salerery is open so we can discus wat you want to pay me and wat you think that I am werth,

I can start imeditely. Thank you in advanse fore yore anser. hopifuly Yore best aplicant so farr.

Sinseerly,

Peggy May Starlings.

Real Job Application Forms

- I procrastinate, especially when the task is unpleasant.
- Personal interests: donating blood. Fourteen gallons so far.As indicted, I have over five years of analyzing investments.
- Instrumental in ruining entire operation for a Midw***est chain store.
- Note: Please don't misconstrue my 14 jobs as job-hopping. I have never quit a job.
- Marital status: Often. Children: Various.
- Reason for leaving last job: They insisted that all employees get to work by 8:45 a.m. every morning. I couldn't work under those conditions.
- The company made me a scapegoat, just like my three previous employers.
- Finished eighth in my class of ten.
- References: none. I've left a path of destruction behind

Resume Bloopers

- Job Duties: "Answer phones, file papers, respond to customer e-mails, take odours."
- Interests: "Gossiping."
- Favourite Activities: "Playing trivia games. I am a repository of worthless knowledge."
- Skills: "I can type without looking at the keyboard."
- Employer: "Myself; received pay rise for high sales."
- Objective: "I want to play a major part in watching a company advance."
- Experience: "Chapter President, 1887-1992."
- Experience: "Demonstrated ability in multi-tasting."
- Experience: "I'm a hard worker, etc."
- Languages: "Speak English and Spinach."
- Reason for leaving: "I thought the world was coming to an end."
- Additional skills: "I am a Notary Republic."
- Skills: "I have integrity so I will not steal office supplies and take them home."
- Objective: "To hopefully associate with a millionaire one day."
- Skills: "I have technical skills that will take your breath away."
- Qualifications: "I have guts, drive, ambition and heart, which is probably more than a lot of the drones that you have working for you."
- Objective: "I need money because I have bills to pay and I would like to have a life, go out partying, please my young wife with gifts, and have a menu entrée consisting of more than soup."
- Qualifications: "Twin sister has accounting degree."
- Skills: "Written communication = 3 years; verbal communication = 5 years."

- Objective: "I would like to work for a company that is very lax when it comes to tardiness."
- Education: "Have repeated courses repeatedly."
- Salary requirements: "The higher the better."
- Salary desired: "Starting overdue to recent bankrupcies. Need large bonus when starting job."
- Bad traits: "I am very bad about time and don't mind admitting it. Having to arrive at a certain hour doesn't make sense to me. What does make sense is that I do the job. Any company that insists upon rigid time schedules will find me a nightmare."
- References: "Bill, Tom, Eric. But I don't know their phone numbers."
- Work experience: "Two years as a blackjack and baccarat dealer. Strong emphasis on customer relations – a constant challenge considering how much money people lose and how angry they can get."
- Personal: "I limit important relationships to people who want to do what I want them to do."
- Objective: "Student today. Vice president tomorrow."
- Accomplishments: "Brought in a balloon artist to entertain the team."
- Reason for leaving: "Pushed aside so the vice president's girlfriend could steal my job."
- Special skills: "I've got a PhD in human feelings."
- Reason for leaving last job: "Bounty hunting was outlawed in my state."
- Experience: "Any interruption in employment is due to being unemployed."
- Objective: "To become Overlord of the Galaxy!"
- Objective: "What I'm looking for in a job: #1) Money #2) Money #3) Money."

- Hobbies: "Mushroom hunting."
- Experience: "Child care provider: Organised activities; prepared lunches and snakes."
- Objective: "My dream job would be as a professional baseball player, but since I can't do that, I'll settle on being an accountant."
- Awards: "National record for eating 45 eggs in two minutes."
- Heading on stationery: "I'd Break Mom's Heart to Work for You!"
- "I am a 'neat nut' with a reputation for being hardnosed. I have no patience for sloppywork, careless mistakes and theft of company time."
- Experience: "Provide Custer Service."
- Experience: "I was brought in as a turnaround consultant to help turn the company around."
- Strengths: "Ability to meet deadlines while maintaining composer."
- Work experience: "Responsibilities included checking customers out."
- Work experience: "Maintained files and reports, did data processing, cashed employees' pay checks."
- Educational background: "High School: Was an incredible experience."
- Resume: "A great management team that has patents with its workers."
- Cover letter: "Experienced in all faucets of accounting."
- Objective: "I am anxious to use my exiting skills."
- Personal: "I am loyal and know when to keep my big mouth shut."
- Job duties: "Filing, billing, printing and coping."
- Application: "Q: In what local areas do you prefer to work?" A: "Smoking."

- Reason for leaving: "Terminated after saying, It would be a blessing to be fired."
- Personal: "My family is willing to relocate. However not to New England (too cold) and not to Southern California (earthquakes). Indianapolis or Chicago would be fine. My youngest prefers Orlando's proximity to Disney World."
- Resume: "I have a lifetime's worth of technical expertise (I wasn't born – my mother simply chose 'eject child' from the special menu."
- Resume: "Spent several years in the United States Navel Reserve."
- Qualifications: "I have extensive experience with foreign accents."
- "I am fully aware of the kind of attention this position requires."
- References: "Please do not contact my immediate supervisor at the company. My colleagues will give me a better reference."
- "Worked in a consulting office where I carried out my own accountant."
- Accomplishments: "My contributions on product launches were based on dreams that I had."
- Career: "I have worked with restraints for the past two years."
- Experience: "My father is a computer programmer, so I have 15 years of computer experience."
- Education: "I have a bachelorette degree in computers."

●

Kids

"Mum," said the little boy, "where did I come from?"

"The stork brought you, dear," was the reply.

"And where did you come from, Mum?"

"The stork brought me too."

"And what about grandma?"

"The stork brought her too."

"Gee," said the little lad, "Doesn't it ever worry you to think that there have been no natural births in our family for three generations?"

•

A cop saw a little boy standing in the pub smoking a cigarette and drinking a pot of beer.

"Why aren't you in school?" he asked.

"Because I'm only four years old," replied the kid.

•

Little Mary stuck her head around the kitchen door, "Hey Mum. Can an eight-year-old get pregnant?"

"Of course not," said the mother.

Mary turned round. "It's okay fell as we can keep playing the game."

•

Little Tommy, aged eight, marched into the living room with an important announcement for his father. "Dad," he said with great seriousness, "I am gonna get married."

His Dad grinned indulgently, "Who to, son?" he asked.

"My girlfriend, Mary, next door."

Mary was also eight and his Dad decided to carry the joke along. "Found a place to live yet?" he asked.

"Well she gets 50 cents pocket money and you give me dollar. So if she moves in with me, we can manage."

His Dad nodded. "Well, $1.50 a week is fine for now, but what will you do, when the kids start to arrive?"

"Don't worry," said Tommy confidently. "We've been lucky so far."

●

Little Johnny had just met the new kid at the playgroup.
"How old are you?"
"I don't know," said the new kid.
"Do women bother you?"
"No"
"Then you are five."

●

One day a little girl was sitting and watching her mother do the dishes at the kitchen sink. She suddenly noticed that her mother had several white hairs. She looked at her mother inquisitively and asked, "Why are some of your hair white Mom?"

She replied, "Well every time that you do something wrong and make me cry or unhappy, one of my hairs turns white."

The girl thought for a moment and then said, "Momma, how come all grandma's hair is white?"

●

Little five-year-old Johnny was in the bathtub, and his mom was washing his hair. She said to him, "Wow, your hair is growing fast! You need a haircut again."

Little Johnny replied, "Maybe you should stop watering it so much."

●

An irate woman burst into the baker's shop and said, "I sent my son in for two pounds of cookies this morning, but when I weighed them there was one pound. I suggest that you check your scale." The baker looked at her calmly for a moment or two and then replied, "Ma'am, I suggest you weigh your son."

●

A small boy went on a school trip to a local church. On the walls, he saw a gallery of photographs of men in uniform. He asked an usher nearby, who they were.

"Those are our boys who died in service."

The younger queried: "Was that the morning service or the evening service?"

●

A father spotted his four-year-old daughter out in the backyard brushing the family dog's teeth.

"What are you doing?" he asked.

"I'm brushing Bruno's teeth," she replied. "Don't worry, I'll put your toothbrush back, like I always have."

●

A drunk was staggering along the road when he saw a woman walking a young child. "Lady," said the drunk, "that is the ugliest kid I've ever seen in my life. God that child is ugly!"

As the drunk wandered off, the woman burst into tears. A milkman went to her rescue.

"What's the matter, madam?" he asked.

"I've just been terribly insulted," sobbed the woman.

"There, there," said the milkman, reaching into his pocket. "Have this tissue to dry your eyes. And here's a banana for the chimp."

●

"I am glad you named me John," said the small boy.

"Why?" asked his mother.

"Because that's what all the kids at school call me."

●

Little brother: "If you broke your arm in two places, what would you do?"

Boy: "I wouldn't go back to those two places; that's for sure."

●

Marry: "What position does your brother play in the school football team?"

John: "I think he's one of the drawbacks."

●

A little girl made a cup of tea for her mother.

"I didn't know you could make tea," said mum taking a sip.

"Yes I boiled some water, added the tea leaves like you do, and then strained it into a cup. But I couldn't find the strainer, so I used the fly swatter."

"What!" exclaimed mum, choking on her tea.

"Oh, don't worry. I didn't use the new fly swatter. I used the old one.

●

A little girl said to her friend, "I am never going to have kids. I hear they take nine months to download."

●

"Your wife used to like to sing and she played the piano a lot, too. Now we don't hear her at all. How's that?"

"She hasn't the time. We have two children."

"Well, well! After all, children are a blessing!"

●

Young Mother: "The doctor thinks the baby looks like me."

Visitor: "Yes, I wanted to say so, but feared you might be offended."

●

"Hey Mum, where do babies come from?"

"From the stork of course."

"But who gets the stork pregnant?"

●

"Mummy, you know the vase you were always worried I would break?"

"Yes"

"Well, your worries are over."

Lawyers

A man went to his lawyer and said, "I would like to make a will but I don't know exactly how to go about it."

The lawyer said, "No problem, leave it all to me." The man looked somewhat upset and said, "Well, I know you were going to take the biggest slice, but I would like to leave a little to my children too."

●

A dog ran into a butcher shop and grabbed a roast off the counter. Fortunately the butcher recognised the dog as belonging to one of his neighbours. The neighbour happened to be a lawyer. Incensed by the theft, the butcher called up his neighbour and said, "Hey, if your dog stole a roast from my shop, would you be liable for the cost of the meat?"

The lawyer replied, "Of course. How much was the roast?"

"$7.98," said the butcher.

A few days later the butcher received a cheque in the mail for $7.98. Attached to it was an invoice that read: "Legal consultation service $150."

●

Two lawyers entered a diner and ordered a couple of drinks. They then took sandwiches from their briefcases and began to eat.

Seeing this, the angry owner went over to them and said, "Excuse me, but you can't eat your own sandwiches in here."

Shrugging their shoulders, the lawyer exchanged sandwiches.

●

Noticing they were having engine trouble, the pilot instructed the crew to tell the passengers to take their seats and prepare for an emergency landing. A few moments later, the pilot asked the attendants if everyone was buckled in and ready.

"We're all set here, captain," an attendant replied, "except for one lawyer, who is still going around passing his business cards.

●

A new client had just come in to see a famous lawyer.

"Can you tell me how much you charge?" said the client.

"Of course." The lawyer replied.

"I charge $200 to answer three questions!"

"Well that's a bit steep, isn't it?"

"Yes it is." said the lawyer. "And what's your third question?"

●

A man walked into a bar with a crocodile and asked, "Do you serve lawyers here?"

"We sure do." The bartender answered.

"Good," the man said. "I'll have a beer and my croc will have a lawyer."

●

"I have some good news and bad news." A defence lawyer told his client. "First the bad news. The blood test came back and your DNA is an exact match with that found at the crime scene."

"Oh, no!" cried the client. What is the good news?"

"Your cholesterol is down to 140."

●

Charged with stealing a barrel of beer from the back of the pub, the old defendant was not familiar with legal jargon. So when the judge said he would have to dismiss the case due to insufficient evidence the old lag scratched his head and said:"What do you mean?"

The clerk explained: "It means you are let off."

"And does it mean I can keep the barrel?" he asked.

●

She was seeking maintenance for her baby.

"Do you know who the father is?" asked the solicitor.

"Yes," she sobbed. "It was Tommy."

"But we can't sue Tommy. Don't you know his surname?"

"No. You see I didn't know him personally."

●

Two New York lawyers hired a secretary from a small town in the hills. She was attractive, but it was obvious that she knew nothing about city life.

One lawyer said to the other, "Mary is so young and pretty she might be taken advantage by some of those fast racing city guys. Why don't we teach her what's right and what is wrong?"

"Great idea," said the partner. "You teach her what's right."

●

A cardiac patient was told that he needed an urgent heart transplant. The surgeon said: "You can have a doctor's heart 10,000 dollars, a rabbi's heart for 20,000 or a lawyer's heart for 100,000."

"Why are lawyers' hearts so expensive?" asked the patient.

"Well," said the surgeon, "we have to go through a lot of lawyers to find a heart."

●

Two boys were talking on their first day in school. "My daddy's an accountant," said one. "What does your daddy do?"

"My daddy's a lawyer."

"Honest?"

"No, just the regular kind."

●

The solicitor told Paddy that if he wanted to be defended in the court the next day, he would need money. But Paddy was broke.

"All I've got is an antique gold watch," he said.

Solicitor: "Well that's all right, you can raise cash on that. Now what are you accused of stealing?"

Paddy: "An antique gold watch!"

●

A lawyer's son wanted to follow in his father's footsteps. He went to law school, graduated with honours and joined his father's law firm. At the end of his first day there, he ran in excitedly to tell his father. "Guess what! On my first day, I cracked that accident case you've been working on for the past four years."

"You idiot!" said the father. "What do you think why I put you through law school?"

●

Fred consulted his lawyer. "I've been receiving threatening letters," he said.

"That's terrible," said the legal eagle. "We'll put a stop to that. Who are they from?"

"The Taxation Department," said Fred.

●

"Have you ever been cross-examined before?"

"Yes, your honour, I'm a married man."

●

"Do you plead guilty or not guilty?"
"What else have you got?"

●

"Guilty. Ten days or two hundred dollars."
"I'll take the two hundred dollars."

●

"Have you anything to offer before judgement is passed?"
"No, judge, my lawyer has left me broke."

●

Judge: You are charged with habitual drunkenness, what is your excuse?"
"Habitual thirst, Your Worship."

●

"Do you plead guilty or not guilty?"
"How do I know? I haven't heard the evidence yet."

●

"Order, order in the court."
"Whisky, on the rocks for me thanks."

●

Boss to pretty secretary: "Just because I made love to you last night, who said you could come in late?"
Secretary: "My solicitor."

●

How many lawyers does it take to change the light bulb?
Three: One to climb the ladder one to shake the ladder and one to sue the ladder company.

●

What is the difference between a lawyer and a sperm?
A sperm has one in a million chance of turning into a human being.

●

What's the difference between a good lawyer and a great lawyer?

A good lawyer knows the law, a great lawyer knows the judge.

●

Why did the post office recall the new layer stamps?
Because people could not tell which side to spit on.

●

What is the difference between a lawyer and a leech?
A leech quits sucking blood after you die.

●

Why did the lawyer cross the road?
To sue the chicken on the other side.

●

Why are lawyers never attacked by sharks?
Professional courtesy.

●

What did the lawyer name his daughter? Sue.

●

Why does the law society prohibit sex between lawyers and their clients?

To prevent clients from being billed twice for essentially the same service.

●

What do lawyers do when they die? Lie still.

●

What do you get if you cross the lawyer with a drunken pig?
Nothing. There are some things a drunk pig won't do.

●

What is the difference between a good lawyer and a bad lawyer?

A bad lawyer can let a case drag out for several years. A good lawyer can make it last even longer.

●

If you were stranded on a desert island with Hitler, Saddam Hussein and a lawyer and you had a gun with only two bullets, what would you do?

Shoot the lawyer twice.

Lawyer Quotes

Do you promise to pay the bill, the total bill and nothing but the bill?

●

A lawyer will do anything to win a case, sometimes he will even tell the truth.

●

Ignorance of the law excuses no man from practising.

●

In almost every case, you have to read between the lies.

●

A lawyer is a gentleman who rescues your estate from your enemies and keeps it for himself.

●

A man is innocent until proved broke.

Mama

- ❑ Your mama is so fat she has to fly cargo class.
- ❑ Your mama is so fat she's got shock absorbers on her toilet seat.
- ❑ Your mama is so fat her driver's licence says: "Picture continued on other side".
- ❑ Your mama is so fat she can't even jump to conclusions.
- ❑ Your mama is so fat she qualifies for group insurance.
- ❑ Your mama is so fat every time she walks in high heels she strikes oil.
- ❑ Your mama is so fat that when she gets into an elevator, it has to go down.

- Your mama is so fat that when she lies on the beach, she's is the only one to get the sun.

- Your mama is so fat that when she steps on the scale, it reads: "One at a time please."
- Your mama is so fat she's got her own area code.
- Your mama is so fat when she sits in front of the Hollywood sign, you can only see the "H" and the "D".
- Your mama is so fat that when she has sex, she has to give directions.
- Your mama is so poor she can't even to pay attention.
- Your mama is so poor, her TV has two channels – on and off.
- Your mama is so stupid she puts lipstick on her forehead to make up her mind.
- Your mama is so stupid she sold her car for petrol money.
- Your mama is so stupid that at the bottom of the application where it says: "Sign here", she writes "Aquarius"
- Your mama is so stupid that when she saw the sign: "Under 18 not admitted", she went home and got 17 friends.
- Your mama is so ugly that when she gets up the sun goes down.
- Your mama is so ugly that when they took her to the beautician, it took 12 hours for a quote.
- Your mama is so ugly that your father takes her to work with him, so that he doesn't have to kiss her goodbye.
- Your mama is so ugly that when she was born, the doctor smacked the wrong end.

- Your mama is so ugly that when she was born, she was put in an incubator with tinted windows.
- Your mama's house is so dirty she has to wipe her feet before she goes out.

Marriage

When a man bringing his wife flowers for no reason, there's a reason.

●

Laugh and the world laughs with you. Quarrel with your wife and you sleep alone.

●

Marriage is the price men pay for sex, and sex is the price women pay for marriage.

●

Marriage is not a word, it is a sentence.

●

Marriage is not a lottery. In a lottery you have a chance.

●

Marriage is like a three-ring circus. First, the engagement ring; second, the wedding ring; and third the suffer-ring.

●

Marriage has its good side. It teaches you loyalty, tolerance, self-restraint and many other qualities you wouldn't need if you stayed single.

●

If a woman does household chores for $250 a week, that is domestic science. If she does it for nothing, that's marriage.

Men

Man to God: "God, why did you make woman so beautiful?"
God: "So that you would love her."
Man: "But why did you make her so dumb?"
God: "So that she would love you."

●

Why did God create woman?
Because after creating man, he was sure he could do better.

●

Men are like bank accounts – without a lot of money, they don't generate much interest.

●

What's the difference between a new husband and a new dog?
After a year, the dog is still excited to see you.

●

How does a man show that he's planning for the future?
He buys two cases of beer instead of one.

●

How do you get a man to exercise?
Tie the TV remote control to his shoelaces.

●

When is the only time a man thinks about a candlelit dinner?
When there is a power cut.

●

Diamonds are a girl's best friend. Dogs are man's best friend.
So which is the dumber sex?

●

What are the three words guaranteed to humiliate men everywhere?
"Hold my purse."

●

The quickest way to a man's heart is through his chest.

●

Men are like vacations: they never seem to last long enough.

●

What's the difference between a savings bond and the typical male?
At some point the savings bond will mature.

●

What's the difference between a man and childbirth?
One is a constant pain and is almost unbearable, the other is simply having a baby.

●

There are "ups" and "downs" in every man's sex life.

●

What do you call a man with half a brain? Gifted.

●

What do you call a handcuffed man? Trustworthy.

●

What's the smallest thing a man can say? "My wife says….."

●

What do you call an intelligent man in America? A tourist.

●

What are two reasons why men don't mind their business?
1. No mind. 2. No business.

●

Why are all dumb jokes one liners? So men can understand them.

●

What do men and mascara have in common?
They both run at the first sign of emotion.

●

What's man's idea of helping with housework?
Lifting his legs so you can vacuum.

●

What should you give a man who has everything?
A woman to show him how to work.

●

The man who can read women like a book usually likes to read in bed.

Men Are Like....

- Bananas: the older they get, the less firm they are.
- Mini skirts: if you're not careful, they'll creep up your legs.
- Cement: after getting laid, they take ages to get hard.
- Computers: hard to figure out and they never have enough memory.
- Commercials: you can't believe a word they say.
- Popcorn: they satisfy you, but only for a short while.
- Snowstorms: you never know when they're coming, how many inches you'll get, or how long they'll last.
- Copiers: you need them for reproduction, but that's about it.
- Coolers: load them with beer and you can take them anywhere.
- Mats: they only show up when there's food on the table.
- Horoscopes: they always tell you what to do and are usually wrong.
- Noodles: they're always in hot water and they lack taste.
- Lava lamps: fun to look at, but not all that bright.
- Parking spots: the good ones are already taken and the ones that are left are handicapped.
- Blenders: you need one, but you're not quite sure why.
- Fragments of soap: they get together in bars.
- Lawn mowers: if you're not pushing one around, then you're riding it.
- Chocolate: sweet, smooth, and they usually go straight to your hips

Mother-in-Law

A lawyer cabled his client overseas: "Your mother-in-law passed away in her sleep. Shall we order a burial or cremation?"

The reply came back: "Take no chances; order both."

●

What is the penalty for bigamy? Two mothers-in-law.

●

The front doorbell rang and a man opened the door to find his mother-in-law on the step with a suitcase.

Can I stay here for a few days?" she asked.

He said, "Sure you can," and shut the door in her face.

●

My mother-in-law broke up my marriage. One day my wife came up early and found us in bed together.

●

A man took his dog to the vet to cut off its tail. The vet wanted to know why.

Because," said the man, "my mother-in-law is arriving tomorrow, and I don't want anything to make her think she's welcome."

●

I said to my mother-in-law, "My house is your house." She said, "Get the hell off my property."

●

A husband was late from work one evening. "I am sure he's having an affair," said his wife to her mother.

"Why do you always think the worst?" said the mother. "Perhaps he's just been in an accident."

●

My wife's mother said, "When you're dead, I'll dance on your grave."

I replied, "Good, I am being buried at sea."

●

Mrs Brigg's mother was in the habit of visiting her daughter too frequently for Mr Brigg's liking. One day when she arrived she found her daughter in tears.

"What's the matter, my dear?" she asked sympathetically.

"Tom has left me," Mrs Briggs sobbed.

"Oh!" said her mother. "Then there must be some other woman. Do you know who she is?"

"Yes! You!" Cried Mrs. Briggs.

●

"You never told me, dear, what was your reason for becoming a teetotaller?"

Well, it was like this. The last time I came home drunk your mother was here, and I saw two of her."

●

Wife: "What have you done with that book *How to Live a Hundred Years*?

Husband: "You don't think I'm going to leave that lying about with your mother in the house, do you?"

●

Mother: "Was Jack intoxicated when he came home last night?"

Daughter: "I didn't notice anything, except that he asked for a mirror to see who he was!"

●

"You are charged," said the magistrate, "with throwing your mother-in-law out of the window. Have you anything to say?"

"Yes your worship. I did it without thinking."

"I quite realise that, my good man, but don't you see how dangerous it was for anyone who might have been passing by at the time?"

●

"If you and your mother keep nagging, you will bring out the animal in me."

"Don't say that, Henry. We're both scared of mice."

●

"Oh dear! Oh, dear!" moaned the wife. "I wish I'd taken mother's advice and never married you."

The husband swung around quickly, and at last found his voice: "Did your mother try to stop you from marrying me?" He demanded.

The wife nodded violently.

A look of deep remorse crossed the man's face. "Heavens!" He cried. "How I've wronged that woman!"

●

"And what proof can you put forward in support of your contention that you were not speeding?" demanded the magistrate.

"I was on my way to visit my mother-in-law," said the motorist.

●

I was out shopping the other day when I saw six women beating up my mother-in-l   As I stood there and watched, her neighbour, who knows me, said, "Well, aren't you going to help?" I replied, "No, six of them are enough."

●

Doctor: "I am sorry that your mother-in-law had a heart attack."

Son-in-law: "That is impossible."

Doctor: "What do you mean, that's impossible?"

Son-in-law: "She doesn't have a heart."

●

Adam and Eve were the happiest and the luckiest, couple in the world, because neither of them had a mother-in-law.

●

Two men were in a pub and one says to his mate, "My mother-in-law is an angel." His friend replies, "You are lucky. Mine is still alive."

●

"My mother-in-law was bitten by a dog yesterday."
"How is she now?"
"She is fine, but the dog died."

●

A woman awakened her husband in the middle of the night and told him, "There's a burglar downstairs in the kitchen and he is eating the cake that mother made for us."

The husband said, "Who shall I call, the police or an ambulance?"

●

Two friends met in the street. "Where are you coming from?" asked Ted.

"The cemetery," answered Jim. "I just buried my mother-in-law."

"Oh, I'm sorry. But what are those scratches on your face?"
"She put up a heck of a fight."

●

It took time, but eventually I developed a special attachment to my mother-in-law. It fitted over her mouth. (Les Dawson)

●

Doctor: "Don't worry your mother-in-law will get up very soon."

Daughter-in-law: "That's what worries me doctor."

●

Have you heard about this man who took his mother-in-law to the zoo and threw her into the crocodile pool? He is now being sued by RSPCA for being cruel to crocodiles.

●

Last night the local peeping Tom knocked on my mother-in-law's door and asked her to shut her blinds.

●

How many mothers-in-law does it take to change the light bulb?

One. She just holds it up and waits for the world to revolve around her.

●

My mother-in-law and I were happy for 20 years.
Then we met each other.

●

What is the worst thing an emergency doctor can tell you after admitting your mother-in-law to the hospital?

"Sir, we were able to save her."

●

Wonderful woman my mother-in-law, 75 years old and never uses glasses.

Drinks straight from the bottle.

Newspapers

Two years before the Gulf War, a female journalist had done a story for her newspaper on gender roles in Kuwait. She had noted that it was the custom for women to walk several yards behind their husbands. But when she returned recently she observed that the roles had been reversed, and that the men now walked several yards behind their wives.

"This is a wonderful news," the journalist enthused to an Arab woman.

Tell me, what enabled women here to achieve this reversal of roles?"

"Land mines."

●

A newspaper photographer was assigned to take a photograph of a huge forest fire. Owing to the density of the smoke at ground level, his editor hired a light aircraft for aerial shots and the photographer was told that the plane would be waiting for him at a small rural airfield.

The photographer drove at top speed to the airfield and saw a small plane warming up on the runway. He raced over to the plane, jumped in and yelled to the pilot: "Let's go! Let's go."

As the aircraft soared into the sky, the photographer issued his instructions. "I want you to fly over the north side of the fire and make three or four low-level passes."

"Why?" asked the pilot.

"What do you mean why?" asked the photographer. "So that I can take pictures. I'm a photographer and photographers take pictures."

The pilot thought for a moment. "So does that mean you're not the instructor?"

●

A reporter saw a crowd gathered around a road accident. Anxious to get a scoop, he told the bystanders, "Let me through! I'm the son of the victim."

The crowd made a way for him. Lying in front of the car was a donkey.

●

There's very little advice in men's magazines because men don't think there's a lot they don't know. Women do. Women want to learn. Men think, "I know what I'm doing, just show me somebody naked." (Jerry Seinfeld)

Old Age

Late on a Friday afternoon, a well-dressed senior citizen walked into a jewellery shop with a pretty, young blonde and she looked at some diamond necklaces. She selected an expensive one and the senior citizen paid by cheque and they walked out.

On Monday, he got a call from the jeweller, "Your cheque bounced, please come and pay or return the necklace." As he went back to return the necklace, the jeweller asked, "So what was the fun of all this?"

The senior citizen replied, "A marvellous weekend."

Exercising After 50

Begin by standing on a comfortable surface, where you have plenty of room on each side.

With a five-pound potato sack in each hand, extend your arms straight out from your sides and hold them there as long as you can.

Try to hold it for a full minute, and then relax. Each day you'll find that you can hold this position for just a bit longer.

After a couple of weeks, move up to 10-pound potato sacks. Then try 50-pound potato sacks and then eventually try to get to where you can lift a 100-pound potato sack in each hand and hold your arms straight for more than a full minute. (I'm at this level.)

After you feel confident at that level, put a potato in each of the sacks.

A reporter was interviewing a 104-year-old woman: "And what do you think is the best thing about being 104 years?" the reporter asked.

She simply replied, "No peer pressure."

A Senior Citizen

I Am A Senior Citizen...

- ❑ I'm the life of the party...even when it lasts till 8pm.
- ❑ I'm very good at opening childproof caps with a hammer.
- ❑ I'm usually interested in going home before I get to where I'm going.
- ❑ I'm good on a trip for at least an hour without my aspirin, antacid...
- ❑ I'm the first one to find the bathroom wherever I go.
- ❑ I'm awake many hours before my body allows me to get up.
- ❑ I'm smiling all the time because I can't hear a word you're saying.
- ❑ I'm very good at telling stories...over and over and over and over.
- ❑ I'm aware that other people's grandchildren are not as bright as mine.
- ❑ I'm so cared for: long-term care, eye care, private care, dental care.
- ❑ I'm not grouchy, I just don't like traffic, waiting, children, politicians...
- ❑ I'm positive I did housework correctly before the Internet.
- ❑ I'm sure everything I can't find is in a secure place.
- ❑ I'm wrinkled, saggy and lumpy, and that's just my left leg.
- ❑ I'm having trouble remembering simple words like... uh...
- ❑ I'm realising that aging is not for sissies.

- I'm walking more (to the bathroom) and enjoying it less.
- I'm sure they are making adults much younger these days.
- I'm wondering, if you're only as old as you feel, how could I be alive at 150?
- I'm anti-everything now: anti-fat, anti-smoke, anti-noise, anti-inflammatory.
- I'm a walking storeroom of facts... I've just lost the key to the storeroom.
- I'm a senior citizen and I think I am having the time of my life... Aren't I?

Philosophy

- If tomorrow never comes, then you're dead.
- Money is the root of all wealth.
- Drilling for oil is boring.
- A beer in the hand is worth two in the fridge.
- The man who gives in when he is wrong, is wise. The man who gives in when he is right, is married.
- Love thy neighbour, but first make sure her husband is away.
- If love is a dream, then marriage is an alarm clock.
- Marriage is one of the chief causes of divorce.
- Where there's a will, make sure you're in it.
- There's no such thing as non-existent.
- Money can't buy everything: that's what credit cards are for.
- It's bad luck to be superstitious.
- One good turn gets most of the blanket.
- If you feel the world is moving fast, take comfort from the queue for the supermarket checkout.
- Your temper is one of the few things that improve the longer you keep it.

- Laughter is the best medicine, unless you are sick. Then you should ring 999.
- Condoms are easier to change than nappies.
- If you want your wife to pay undivided attention to every word you say, talk in your dream.
- Beat the five o'clock rush; leave work at noon.
- Always use tasteful words; you may have to eat them.
- If you can't beat them, arrange to have them beaten.
- The best way to keep the wolf from the door is to leave a sheep in the garden.
- If you can smile when things go wrong, you have someone in mind to blame.
- Borrow money from pessimists; they don't expect it back.
- If you think nobody cares about you, try missing a couple of mortgage payments.
- Nothing in the known universe travels faster than a bad cheque.
- A fool and his money are soon partying.
- If money could talk, it would say goodbye.
- Work is a fine thing if it doesn't take too much of your spare time.
- The easiest way to find something lost around the house is to buy a replacement.
- Smile – it makes people wonder what you're thinking.
- Never take life seriously. Nobody gets out alive anyway.
- A penny for some people's thoughts is still a fair price.
- God made the pot. Man made the beer. Who do you trust?
- A day without sunshine is like….night.
- First impressions are often lasting; especially if they're made by car number.
- If everything isn't going your way, you're driving in the wrong lane.
- A clear conscience is usually the sign of a bad memory.

- When two egotists meet, it's I for I.
- An escalator can never break, it can only become stairs.
- Don't hate yourself in the morning; sleep till noon.
- Practise safe eating: use condiments.
- Do not argue with your spouse when she is packing your parachute.
- Teamwork is essential; it allows you to blame someone else.
- Always talk to your wife while making love – if there's phone handy.
- Alcohol is not the answer; it makes you forget the question.
- Sea captains don't like crew cuts.
- A bird in the hand makes blowing your nose difficult.
- Early to rise and early to bed makes a man healthy but socially dead.
- The road to success is always under construction.
- There is no such thing as absolute truth. This is absolutely true.
- It's not hard to meet expenses – they are everywhere.
- Nobody is ugly after 2 a.m.
- A bird in the hand is safer than one overhead.
- Sex is not the answer. Sex is the question. The answer is "yes".
- Talk is cheap till lawyers get involved.
- The trouble with half-truths is that you never know which half you've got.
- Wink till she's cute, but stop before the wedding.
- When a man talks dirty to a woman, it's sexual harassment. When a woman talks dirty to a man, it $5.95 a minute.
- Sex is like air; it's not important unless you aren't getting it.
- Change is inevitable, except from the vending machine.
- He who laughs last, thinks slowest.
- Hard work has a future payoff, but laziness pays off now.

Politics

Hillary Clinton was out walking near the White House one day when she saw a young boy trying to selling puppies.

"My, they're so cute." Said the First Lady.

"And they're all Democrats," replied the boy.

"Is that so?" said Hillary. "I tell you. I'm so taken with these puppies that if you've got one left at the weekend, I'm going to buy one."

The following weekend, Hillary passed the same spot and saw the boy with just two puppies left.

"I'd like to buy one," she said. "How much?"

"Fifty dollars each," said the boy. "They're both Republicans."

"Wait a minute," snapped Hillary. "The other day you said they were Democrats."

"Well, yes, ma'am," answered the boy. "But since then they've opened their eyes."

●

A busload of politicians was speeding along a country road when it ploughed into a tree and overturned. There was blood and glass everywhere. An old farmer saw the crash and was first on the scene. Within two hours, he had dug a huge hole and buried all the politicians.

A few days later, the local sheriff was passing through when he saw the wreckage of the bus. The farmer explained what had happened.

"Were they all dead?" inquired the sheriff.

"Well," said the farmer. "Some of them said they weren't, but you know how the politicians lie."

●

When a little boy desperately needed $100 to buy a present, his mother suggested that he pray for it. So he wrote to God asking for the money. The Post Office intercepted the letter and forwarded it to the President who was so touched by the request that he instructed his secretary to send the boy $5.

On receiving the money, the boy wrote back: "Dear God, Thank you very much for sending me the money, I noticed that you had sent it through Washington. As usual, those thieving bastards deducted $95 dollars."

●

One day George Bush was out jogging and accidentally fell from a bridge into a very cold river. Three boys playing along the river saw the accident. Without a second thought, they jumped into the water and dragged the wet President out of the river.

After cleaning up he said, "Boys, you saved the President of the United States today. You deserve a reward."

The first boy said, "I'd like a ticket to Disneyland."

"I'll personally hand it to you," said Mr. Bush

"I would like a pair of Nike Air Turbos," said the second boy.

"I'll buy them myself and give them to you," said the grateful Bush.

"I'd like a wheelchair with a stereo in it," said the third boy.

"I'll personally...wait a second, son, you are not handicapped!"

"No....But I will be when my dad finds out that I saved you from drowning."

●

How long does an Indian politician serve? Till he gets caught.

●

A life supporter of the Labour Party was lying on his deathbed when he suddenly decided to join the Tory Party.

"But why?" asked a puzzled friend, "You are Labour through and through.

"Why change now?"

The man leaned forward and explained, "Well, I'd rather like it was one of them that died, not one of us."

●

An official Gallup Poll polled over 1,000 women with the question: "Would you sleep with former US President Bill Clinton?"

1% said "No"

2% said "Yes"

97% said "Never again."

●

While on safari in cannibal country a traveller came across a café in a clearing in the jungle. The sign in front advertised: "Fried Missionary $5, Boiled Hunter $4.50, Grilled Safari Guide $6, Stuffed Politician $15."

When the traveller asked, "Why so much for a politician?" the chef replied, "Have you ever tried to clean one?"

●

He walked into the general store of a country town and bought all the rotten fruit, tomatoes and eggs available. The greengrocer beamed: "I bet you are going to hear the visiting MP at the Royal Hall tonight."

"No," he replied. "I AM the visiting MP!"

●

The proposition to put a king-sized statue of the Prime Minister in the Central Park has been well supported. It will give shelter when it's raining, shade in the summer, and will give the pigeons a chance to speak for us all.

●

"Mr. Minister!" boomed a back-bencher, "What are you going to do about the Abortion bill?"

"Shhh, not so loud," said the Minister, "I'm paying it tomorrow."

●

No matter who you vote for, a darned politician always wins. And the only thing wrong with political jokes is that they get elected.

●

Make your MP work; Don't re-elect him.

●

Politicians are the same all over. They promise to build bridges, even when there are no rivers.

●

Artificial hearts are nothing new. Politician had them for years.

●

Capitalism is the exploitation of man by man. Socialism is the exact opposite.

Political Definitions

Capitalism: You possess two cows. You sell one and buy a bull.

Socialism: You possess two cows. You give one of them to your neighbour.

Communism: You possess two cows. The government confiscates them and provides you with milk.

Nazism: You possess two cows. The government confiscates them and shoots you.

European Union: You possess two cows. The government confiscates them, shoots one, milks the other and pours it down the drain.

Proverbs

A junior schoolteacher gave her class the first halves of well-know proverbs and asked the children to complete them.

These are the authentic answers:

- Where there is smoke, there's.... pollution.
- A penny saved is....not much.
- Don't count your chickens....eat them.
- Better to be safe than.... punch a fifth former.
- Too many cooks....so few meals.
- Don't bite the hand that... looks dirty.
- Two's company. Three's.... the Musketeers.
- Laugh and the world laughs with you; cry and....you have to blow your nose.
- Strike while the ....bug is close.
- Look before you... run into a pole.
- An idle mind is.... the best way to relax.
- Happy the bride who...gets all the presents.
- If you lie down with dogs you'll.... stink in the morning.
- There's no fool like....Aunt Edie.
- A watched pot....never disappears.
- If you can't stand the heat ...get a pool.
- You can't teach an old dog new... maths.
- Children should be seen and not...spanked.
- A miss is as good as a.... mister.

Quotations

Age

You know you are getting old when the candles cost more than the cake.
(Bob Hope)

●

Age is strictly a case of mind over the matter. If you don't mind, it doesn't matter.
(Jack Benny)

●

The secret of staying young is to live honestly, eat slowly and lie about your age.
(A. Adam)

●

One should never trust a woman who tells her real age. If she tells that, she'll tell anything.
(Oscar Wilde)

●

As you get older three things happen. The first is your memory goes and I can't remember the other two...
(Sir Norman Wisdom)

●

Wrinkle should merely indicate where smiles have been.
(Mark Twain)

●

It takes a long time to become young. *(Pablo Picasso)*

●

Like many women of my age, I am 28 years old.
(Mary Schmich)

●

I refuse to admit I'm more than 52 even if that does make my sons illegitimate.
(Lady Astor)

●

Whenever the talk turns to age, I say I am 49 plus VAT.
(Lionel Blair)

●

Youth has no age.   *(Pablo Picasso)*

●

Old men are dangerous it doesn't matter to them what is going to happen to the world.   *(George Bernard Shaw)*

●

Whenever a man's friends begin to compliment him about looking young, he may be sure that they think he is growing old.   *(Washington Irving)*

●

It is strange that the one thing that every person looks forward to, namely old age, is the one thing for which no preparation is made.   *(John Dewy)*

Books

There are books of which the back and covers are by far the best parts.   *(Charles Dickens)*

●

A good novel tells the truth about its hero; but a bad novel tells the truth about its author.   *(G. K. Chesterton)*

●

A man's got to take a lot of punishment to write a really funny book.   *(Ernest Hemingway)*

●

Some books are undeservedly forgotten; none are undeservedly remembered.   *(W. H. Auden)*

●

You don't have to burn books to destroy a culture. Just get people to stop reading them   *(Ray Bradbury)*

●

It was a book to kill time for those who like it better dead.   *(Dame Rose Macaulay)*

●

Books are good enough in their own way, but they are a mighty bloodless substitute for life.

(Robert Louis Stevenson)

●

Books do furnish a room.   *(Anthony Powell)*

●

A library is thought in cold storage.   *(Lord Samuel)*

●

Before you be not swallowed up in books! An ounce of it is worth a pound of knowledge.   *(John Wesley)*

●

Learning hath gained most by those books by which the printers have lost.   *(T. Fuller)*

Children

The trouble with the children is that they're not returnable.
(Quentin Crisp)

●

The first half of our life is ruined by our parents and the second half by our children.   *(Clarence Darrow)*

●

Children really brighten up the household; they never turn the lights off.   *(Ralph Bus)*

●

Having one child makes you a parent; having two you are a referee.   *(David Frost)*

●

Children aren't happy with nothing to ignore. And that's what parents were created for. (Ogden Nash)

●

I love children – especially when they cry, for then someone takes them away. (Michel de Montaigne)

●

The proper time to influence the character of a child is about a hundred years before he is born.

(William Ralph Inge)

●

Never have children, only grandchildren.

(Gore Vidal)

●

Experts say you should never hit children in anger. When is a good time? When you are feeling festive.

(Barr Roseanne)

●

I have got seven kids, the three words you hear most around my house are: "Hello", goodbye", and "I am pregnant".

(Dean Martin)

Computers
They've finally come up with the perfect office computer. It makes a mistake, it blames another computer.

(Milton Berle)

●

Reading computer manuals for the hardware is as frustrating as reading sex manuals without the software.

(Arthur. C. Clarke)

●

Computers are useless. They can only give you answers.

(Pablo Picasso)

●

Computers will never take the place of books. You can't stand on the floppy disk to reach a high shelf.

(Sam Ewing)

●

To err is human, but to really foul things up you need a computer.

(Paul Ehrlich)

●

All sorts of computer errors are now turning up. You would be surprised to know the number of doctors who claim they are treating pregnant men.

(Issac Asimov)

●

I don't fear the computer. I fear the lack of it.

(Issac Asimov)

●

The only way to make your PC go faster is to throw it out of a window.

(Paul Ehrlich)

Drink

No animal ever invented anything as bad as drunkenness or as good as drink.

(G. K. Chesterton)

●

I envy people who drink – at least they know what to blame everything on.

(Oscar Levant)

●

I've never been drunk, but I've often been over-served.

(George Gobel)

●

You can tell German wine from vinegar by the label.

(Mark Twain)

●

Anybody who hates dogs and loves whisky can't be all bad.

(W. C. Fields)

●

When I read about the evils of drinking, I gave up reading.
(Henry Youngman)

●

A man's got to believe in something. I believe I'll have another drink. *(W. C. Fields)*

●

You are not drunk if you can lie on the floor without holding on. *(Dean Martin)*

●

Actually, it only takes one drink to get loaded. The trouble is, I can't remember if it is the thirteenth or fourteenth.
(George Burns)

●

A drink a day keeps the shrink away.
(Edward Abbey

●

I saw a notice which said "Drink Canada Dry" and I've just started. *(Brendan Behan)*

●

Mary was a woman who drove to me to drink. I never had the courtesy to thank her. *(W. C. Fields)*

●

Don't put ice in my drink: it takes too much room.
(Groucho Marx)

God

God is a comedian playing to an audience too afraid to laugh. *(Voltaire)*

●

God heals and the doctor takes the fees.
(Benjamin Franklin)

●

Is man one of the God's blunders, or is God one of man's blunders?   *(Freidrich Nietzsche)*

•

God writes a lot of comedy...the trouble is he's stuck with so many bad actors who don't know how to play funny.
                                                        (Garrision Keillor)

•

If you want to make God laugh, tell him your future plans.
                                                        (Woody Allen)

•

It is the final proof of God's omnipotence that he need not exist in order to save us.   *(William Cowper)*

•

God is a circle whose centre is everywhere and whose circumference is nowhere.   *(William Cowper)*

•

The body of a young woman is God's greatest achievement. Of course He could have made it last longer, but you can't have everything.   *(Neil Simon)*

•

In the first place, God made idiots: that was for practice; then He made school boards.   *(Mark Twain)*

•

If only God would give me some clear sign! Like making a large deposit in my name at a Swiss bank.   *(Agathon)*

•

They say God has existed from the beginning of time and will exist beyond the end of time. Can you imagine trying to sit through his home movies?   *(Scott Roeben)*

•

If the concept of God has any validity or any use, it can only be to make us larger, freer and more loving. If God cannot do this, then it is time we got rid of Him.   *(Agathon)*

•

God seems to have left the receiver off the hook, and time is running out. *(Arthur Koestler)*

Government

I don't make jokes: I just watch the government and report the facts. *(Rogers Will)*

•

Governments never learn. Only people learn.

(Milton Friedman)

•

The danger is not that a particular class is unfit to govern. Every class is unfit to govern. *(Lord Acton)*

•

Governments don't retreat, they simply advance in another direction. *(Geoffrey Rippon)*

•

Government is like a baby. An alimentary canal with a big appetite at one end and no sense of responsibility at the other. *(Ronald Reagan)*

•

Folks who don't know why America is the land of promise, should be here during an election campaign. *(Milton Berle)*

•

Recession is when your neighbour loses his job. Depression is when you lose yours. And recovery is when Jimmy Carter loses his. *(Ronald Reagan)*

•

Giving money and power to governments is like giving whisky and the car keys to teenage boys. *(P. J. Orourke)*

•

Britain has invented a new missile. It's called the civil servant; it doesn't work and it can't be fired.

(Walter Walker)

It is true that you can't fool all the people all the time, but you can fool enough of them to rule a large country.

(Will Durant)

•

In governments there must be both shepherds and butchers.   *(Voltaire)*

•

Man is not the enemy of Man, but through the medium of a false system of government.   *(Thomas Paine)*

•

Anarchy may not be the best form of government, but it's better than no government at all.   *(Anonymous)*

Happiness

Some people cause happiness wherever they go; others, whenever they go.   *(Oscar Wilde)*

•

A man doesn't know what happiness is till he is married. By then it is too late.   *(Frank Sinatra)*

•

The pursuit of happiness is a most ridiculous phrase; if you pursue happiness you'll never find it.   *(C. P. Snow)*

•

Happiness is a very small desk and a very big wastebasket.

(Robert Orben)

•

Happiness is like a kiss. You must share it to enjoy it.

(Bernard Meltzer)

•

One of the keys to happiness is a bad memory.

(Rita Mae Brown)

•

Happiness is no laughing matter.   *(Richard Whatley)*

•

Happiness is a good bank account, a good cook and a good digestion.   *(Jean Jacques Rousseau)*

•

A lifetime of happiness! No man alive could bear it: it would be hell on earth.   *(George Bernard Shaw)*

•

The happiest women, like the happiest nations, have no history.   *(George Eliot)*

•

Happiness? A good cigar, a good meal and a good woman...or a bad woman; it depends on how much happiness you can handle.   *(George Burns)*

•

Happiness is good health and a bad memory.
(Ingrid Bergman)

•

If you want to understand the meaning of happiness you must see it as a reward and not as a goal.
(Antoine de Saint-Exupery)

•

O, how better a thing it is to look into happiness through another man's eyes.   *(William Shakespeare)*

•

If you ask yourself whether you are happy, you cease to be so.   *(John Stuart Mill)*

•

Had I been brighter, the ladies been gentler, the Scotch been weaker, had God been kinder, had the dice been hotter, this could have been a one sentence story: Once upon a time I lived happily ever after.   *(Mickey Rooney)*

•

Life

Life's tragedy is that we get old too soon and wise too late. *(Benjamin Franklin)*

●

Life is a tragedy when seen in close-up, but a comedy in long-shot. *(Charlie Chaplin)*

●

Life is a tragedy full of joy. *(Bernard Malamud)*

●

There is no cure for birth and death, save to enjoy the interval. *(George Santayana)*

●

We are all in the gutter, but some of us are looking at the stars. *(Oscar Wilde)*

●

Life is pleasant. Death is peaceful. It is transition that's troublesome. *(James Byron)*

●

We live in an age when a pizza gets to your home before the police. *(Jeff Mander)*

●

In the end everything is a gag. *(Charlie Chaplin)*

●

What some people mistake for the high cost of living is really the cost of high living. *(Doug Larson)*

●

I enjoy life. I think I'll enjoy death even more. *(Cat Stevens)*

●

Life is too short for chess. *(Henry James Byron)*

●

In three words, I can sum up everything I've learned about life: it goes on. *(Robert Frost)*

●

Life can only be understood backwards; but it must be lived forward. *(Soren Kierkegaard)*

●

I want to live till I die, no more no less.

(Eddie Izzard)

●

When you lie down with a dog, you get up with fleas.·

(Jean Harlow)

●

Life would be tolerable but for its amusements.

(Sir George Lewis)

●

Life is one long process of getting tired.

(Samuel Butler)

●

Oh, isn't life a terrible thing, thank God?

(Dylan Thomas)

●

Life is so short, and there's so much to do, one can't afford to waste a minute; and just think how much you waste, for instance, in walking from place to place instead of going by bus and in going by bus instead of by taxi.

(W. Somerset Maugham)

Love

I recently read that love is entirely a matter of chemistry. That must be why my wife treats me like toxic waste.

(David Bissonnette)

●

If love is blind, why is lingerie so popular? *(Unknown)*

●

Gravitation cannot be held responsible for people falling in love. *(Albert Einstein)*

●

Funny thing how you first meet the woman that you marry. I met my wife in a tunnel of love. She was digging it.
(Les Dawson)

●

Love: a temporary insanity curable by marriage.
(Robert Frost)

●

What the world really needs is more love and less paperwork. *(Peal Bailey)*

●

Love is an irresistible desire to be irresistibly desired.
(Robert Frost)

●

I've been in love with the same woman for forty years. If my wife finds out, she'll kill me. *(Harry Youngman)*

●

Love is like any other luxury. You have no right to it unless you can afford it. *(Anthony Trollope)*

●

There is always some madness in love. But there is also always some reason in madness.
(Friedrich Wilhelm Nietzsche)

●

If love is the answer, could you rephrase the question?
(Lily Tomlin)

●

Absence: that's a common cure for love.
(Miguel De Cervantes)

●

The best love affairs are those we never had.

(Norman Lindsay)

●

Love is that you are the knife which I plunge into myself.

(Franz Kafka)

●

They say that love takes wit away from those who have it, and gives it to those who have none.   *(Denis Diderot)*

●

Love's pleasure only lasts a moment; love's sorrow lasts one's whole life.   *(Jean-Pierre Claris de Florian)*

●

Experience shows us that love is not looking into one another's eyes but looking together in the same direction.

(Antoine de Saint-Exupery)

Marriage

All marriages are happy. It's trying to live together afterwards that causes the problem.   *(Shelly Winters)*

●

All the unhappy marriages come from the husbands having brains. What good are the brains to a man? They only unsettle him.   *(P. G. Woodhouse)*

●

Though women are angels, yet wedlock's the devil.

(Lord Byron)

●

A man in love is incomplete until he has married. Then he's finished.   *(Zsa Zsa Gabor)*

●

Marriage 2001-style, as I know to my cost, is entirely expendable; more easily disposable than a McDonald's wrapper.   *(Vanessa Feltz)*

●

What is the difference between marriage and prison?
In prison somebody else does the cooking.

(Andrea Newman)

●

The most happy marriage I can picture or imagine to myself
would be the union of a deaf man to a blind woman.

(Samuel Taylor Coleridge)

●

It is a sad fact that 50 per cent of marriages in this country
end in divorce. But the other half end in death. You could be
one of the lucky ones. *(Richard Jeni)*

●

In many instances, marriage vows should be more
accurate if the phrase are changed to "Until debt do us part".

(Sam Ewing)

●

Marriage can be viewed as the waiting room for death.

(Mike Myers)

●

The secret of a happy marriage remains a secret.

(Henry Youngman)

●

Always get married early in the morning. That way, if it
doesn't work out, you haven't wasted a whole day.

(Mickey Rooney)

●

A girl must marry for love, and keep on marrying until she
finds it. *(Zsa Zsa Gobor)*

●

All tragedies are finished by a death, all comedies by
marriage. *(Lord Byron)*

●

Marriage is give and take. You'd better give to her or she'll take it anyway.

●

Keep you eyes open before marriage, and half shut afterwards. *(Benjamin Franklin)*

●

After marriage, husband and wife become two sides of a coin; they just can't face each other, but still they stay together. *(Hemant Joshi)*

●

By all means marry, if you get a good wife, you'll be happy. If you get a bad one, you will become a philosopher. *(Socrates)*

●

They say marriages are made in heaven. But so is the thunder and lightning. *(Clint Eastwood)*

●

Where there is marriage without love, there will be love without marriage. *(Benjamin Franklin)*

●

In olden days sacrifices were made at the altar: a practice that still continues. *(Helen Rowland)*

●

I think men who have pierced ear are better prepared for marriage. They have experienced pain and bought jewellery. *(Rita Rudner)*

●

My husband and I didn't sign a pre-nuptial agreement. We signed a mutual suicide. *(Roseanne Barr)*

●

I know nothing about sex because I was always married. *(Zsa Zsa Gabor)*

●

When a man opens a car door for his wife, it's either a new car or a new wife.

(Prince Philip, the Duke of Edinburgh)

●

I sometimes thought of marrying, and then I thought again.

(Noel Coward)

●

Men marry women with the hope they will never change. Women marry men with the hope they will change. Invariably they are both disappointed. *(Albert Einstein)*

●

I am the only man who had the marriage licence made out To Whom It May Concern. *(Mickey Rooney)*

●

I had a bad luck with both of my wives. The first one left me and second one didn't. *(Patrick Murray)*

●

Being a husband is a whole-time job. That is why so many husbands fail. They cannot give their entire attention to it.

(Arnold Bennett)

●

Husbands and wife are one, and that one is the husband.

(Sir William Blackstone)

●

There's only one way to have a happy marriage and as soon as I learn what it is, I'll get married again.

(Clint Eastwood)

●

Husbands are like fires. They go out when unattended.

(Zsa Zsa Gabor)

●

Not all women give most waking thoughts to the problem of pleasing men. Some are married. *(Emma Lee)* ·

●

When you see who some girls marry, you realise how much they must hate to work for a living. *(Helen Rowland)*

●

When you want to marry someone, go have lunch with his ex-wife. *(Shelly Winters)*

●

My mother said it was simple to keep a man: you must be maid in the living room, a cook in the kitchen and a whore in the bedroom. I said I'd hire the other two and take care of the bedroom bit. *(Jerry Hall)*

●

I never married because I have three pets at home that answer the same purpose as a husband. I have a dog that growls every morning. I have parrot that swears all afternoon and a cat that comes late at night. *(Marie Corelli)*

●

Men

I am not denying that women are foolish: God Almighty made them to match with the men. *(George Eliot)*

●

Most women set out to try to change a man, and when they have changed him, they don't like him.

(Cyril Connolly)

●

If men know how women pass the time when they are alone, they'd never marry. *(O. Henry)*

●

If men could get pregnant, abortion would be sacrament.
(Florence Kennedy)

●

Talk to a man about himself, and he will listen for hours.
(Benjamin Disraeli)

●

Bad men live that they may eat and drink whereas good men eat and drink that they may live.   (*Socrates*)

•

I am a marvellous housekeeper. Every time I leave a man I keep his house.   (*Zsa Zsa Gabor*)

•

A successful man is one who makes more money than his wife can spend. A successful woman is one who can find such a man.   (*Lana Turner*)

•

There are only two kinds of men: the dead and the deadly.   (*Helen Rowland*)

•

A man in the house is worth two in the street.   (*Mae West*)

•

Man is a figment of God's imagination.   (*Mark Twain*)

•

Man has his will: but woman has her way.   (*Oliver Wendell Holmes*)

•

When women go wrong, men go right after them.   (*Mae West*)

•

Years ago, manhood was an opportunity for achievement, and now it is a problem to overcome.   (*Garrison Keillor*)

•

A woman needs a man like a fish needs a bicycle.   (*Gloria Steinem*)

•

The true man wants two things: danger and play. For that reason he wants woman, as the most dangerous plaything.   (*Friedrich Nietzsche*)

•

God must love the common man. He made so many of them.   *(Abraham Lincoln)*

●

Money

You can be young without money but you can't be old.
                                   (Tennessee Williams)

●

The two most beautiful words in the English language are 'Cheque enclosed'.   *(Dorthy Parker)*

●

Money won't buy happiness, but it will pay the salaries of a large research staff to study the problem.
                                   (Bill Vaughan)

●

Money is like manure. If you spread it, it does a lot of good but if you pile it up in one place, it stinks like hell.
                                   (Clint W. Murchison)

●

Money couldn't buy you friends, but you get a better class of enemy.   *(Spike Milligan)*

●

Money is just the poor man's credit card.
                                   (Marshall Mc Luhan)

●

Money doesn't talk, it swears.   *(Bob Dylan)*

●

People say that money is not the key to happiness, but I always figured if you have enough money, you can have a key made.   *(Joan Rivers)*

●

Money speaks sense in a language all nations understand.
                                   (Aphra Behn)

●

A man who has £50,000 left when he dies is a failure.
(Errol Flynn)

●

The safe way to double your money is to fold it over once and put it in your pocket. *(Frank Hubbard)*

●

My problem lies in reconciling my gross habits with my net income. *(Errol Flynn)*

●

When it is a question of money, everybody is of the same religion. *(Voltaire)*

●

If you would know what the Lord God thinks of money, you have only to look at those to whom He gives it.
(Maurice Baring)

●

Those who have some means think that the most important thing in the world is love. The poor people know that it is money. *(Gerald Brenan)*

●

Make money: make it honestly if possible; if not, make it by any means. *(Horace)*

●

Money is a good thing for bribing yourself through the inconveniences of life. *(Gottfried Reinhart)*

●

Do you think that when they asked George Washington for his ID that he just whipped out a quarter?
(Stephen Wright)

●

Every day I get up and look through the list of the richest people in America. If I'm not there, I go to work.
(Robert Orban)

●

If you can actually count your money you are not a rich man.
(J. Paul. Getty)

•

Politics

Politics is supposed to be the second oldest profession. I have to realise that it bears a very close resemblance to the first.
(Ronald Reagan)

•

In politics an absurdity is not a handicap.
(Napoleon Bonaparte)

•

Politics is not a bad profession. If you succeed there are many reward, if you disgrace yourself you can always write a book.
(Ronald Reagan)

•

I am not a member of any well-organised political party, I am a Democratic.
(Will Rogers)

•

My choice early in life was either to be a piano player in a whorehouse or a politician. And to tell the truth, there is hardly any difference.
(Harry S. Truman)

•

A politician is a fellow who will lay down your life for his country.
(Texas Guinan)

•

He knows nothing; and he thinks he knows everything. That points clearly to a political career.
(George Bernard Shaw)

•

You can always get the truth from an American statesman after he has turned 70 or given up all hopes of the Presidency.
(Wendell Philipps)

•

Politics is the art of preventing people from becoming involved in affairs which concern them.   *(Paul Valery)*

•

A statesman is a politician who's been dead ten or fifteen years.   *(Harry S. Truman)*

•

Damn your principle; stick to your party.
    (Benjamin Disraeli)

•

We would like to vote for the best man but he is never a candidate.   *(Frank Hubbard)*

•

Half the truth is better than no politics.
    (G. K. Chesteron)

•

I have orders to be awakened at any time in the case of a national emergency, even if I'm in a cabinet meeting.
    (Ronald Reagan)

•

If the Republicans stop telling lies about us, we will stop telling the truth about them.   *(Adlai Stevenson)*

•

I have often wanted to drown my troubles, but I can't get my wife to go swimming.   *(Jimmy Carter)*

•

I have come to the conclusion that politics is too serious a matter to be left to the politicians.   *(Charles de Gaulle)*

•

Politics is perhaps the only profession for which no preparation is thought necessary. *(Robert Louis Stevenson)*

•

Tony Blair is like an actor who doesn't really believe in his script himself but has the incredible skill to make everyone else believe in it.   (*Tom Conti*)

●

Everything is changing. People are taking the comedians seriously and the politicians as a joke.   (*Will Rogers*)

●

One of the penalties for refusing to participate in politics is that you end up being governed by your inferiors. (*Plato*)

●

A liberal is a man too broadminded to take his own side in a quarrel.   (*Robert Frost*)

●

Politics is the art of the possible.   (*Prince Bismarck*)

●

Politics is both fraud and vision.
                                (*Donald Richmond Horne*)

●

Being the President is like a jackass in a hailstorm. There's nothing to do but stand there and take it.
                                (*Lyndon B. Johnson*)

Sex

Sex is a nature and I believe in going along with nature.
                                (*Marilyn Monroe*)

●

If sex is such a natural phenomenon, how come there are so many books on sex?   (*Bette Midler*)

●

Sex appeal is 50 per cent what you've got and 50 per cent what people think you've got.

●

My girlfriend always laugh during sex... no matter what she's reading. *(Steve Jobs)*

●

I admit, I have a tremendous sex drive. My friend lives forty miles away. *(Phyllis Diller)*

●

Sex is one of the nine reasons for reincarnation...The other eight are unimportant. *(Henry Miller)*

●

Continental people have a sex life; the English have hot water bottles. *(George Mikes)*

●

The more sex becomes a non-issue in people's lives, the happier they are. *(Shirley Maclaine)*

●

Reading about sex in yesterday's novels is like watching people smoke in old times. *(Fay Weldon)*

●

Women need a reason to have sex. Men need a place. *(Nora Ephron)*

●

Sex is God's joke on human beings. *(Bette Davis)*

●

I believe that sex is the most beautiful, natural, and wholesome thing that money can buy. *(Steve Martin)*

●

I am a terrible lover: I have actually given a woman an anticlimax. *(Scott Roeben)*

●

The pleasure is momentary, the position ridiculous, and the expense damnable. *(Lord Chesterfield)*

●

It is one of the superstitions of the human mind to have imagined that virginity could be a virtue.   *(Voltaire)*

•

It is hard for me to get used to these changing times. I can remember when the air was clean and sex was dirty.
(George Burns)

Wisdom

Wise men don't take advice. Fools won't take it.
(Benjamin Disraeli)

•

Be wisely worldly, not worldly wise.

(Francis Quarles)

•

My idea of an agreeable person is a person who agrees with me.   *(Benjamin Disraeli)*

•

Some folks are wise, and some are otherwise.
(Tobias Smollett)

•

Knowledge speaks, but wisdom listens.   *(Jimi Hendrix)*

•

The pen is mightier than the sword, and considerably easier to write with.   *(Marty Feldman)*

•

A word to the wise is not necessary – it's the stupid that needs the advice.   *(Bill Cosby)*

•

An appeaser is one who feeds a crocodile – hoping it will eat him last.   *(Winston Churchill)*

•

You are fooling yourself if you argue with the fool: others may not know the difference.　　　　*(Robert Paul)*

●

I believe in getting into hot water. I think it keeps you clean.　　　　*(G. K. Chesterton)*

●

Be wiser than other people if you can, but don't tell them so.　　　　*(Lord Chesterfield)*

●

That man is wisest who, like Socrates, has realised that in truth his wisdom is worth nothing.　　　　*(Plato)*

●

Every generalisation is dangerous, especially this one.
　　　　(Mark Twain)

●

Give a man fish and he eats for a day. Teach him how to fish and you get rid of him all weekend.
　　　　(Zenna Schaffer)

●

The difference between the right word and the almost right is the difference between lightning and a lightning bug.
　　　　(Mark Twain)

●

Knowledge is proud that he has learned so much. Wisdom is humble that he knows no more.　　　　*(William Cowper)*

●

The wise man is not the man who gives the right answers; he is the one who asks the right questions.
　　　　(Claude Levi-Strauss)

●

It is a fine thing even for the old man to learn wisdom.
　　　　(Aeschylus)

●

One may learn wisdom even from one's enemies.

(Aristophanes)

•

No wise man ever wished to be younger.

(Jonathan Swift)

•

A wise man will make more opportunities than he finds.

(Francis Bacon)

•

Why don't they make the whole plane out of that black box stuff?

(Steven Wright)

•

A candidate is someone who gets money from the rich and votes from the poor to protect them from each other.

(Unknown)

Women

There are only two types of women: goddesses and doormats.

(Pablo Picasso)

•

A man can be happy with any woman as long as he does not love her.

(Oscar Wilde)

•

Brigands demand your money or your life; women require both.

(Samuel Butler)

•

Good women keep a diary; the bad never have the time.

(Tallulah Bankhead)

•

With women, the heart argues, not the mind.

(Matthew Arnold)

•

But what is woman? Only one of Nature's agreeable blunders. *(Hannah Cowley)*

●

Frailty, thy name is woman! *(William Shakespeare)*

●

Why would I make one woman so miserable when I can make so many women happy? *(Benny Hill)*

●

If women did not exist, all the money in the world would have no meaning. *(Aristotle Onassis)*

●

Once a woman has given you her heart you can never get rid of the rest of her. *(Sir John Vanbrugh)*

●

Women are like elephants, I like to watch them, but I wouldn't want to own one. *(W. C. Fields)*

●

A woman's mind is cleaner than a man's. She changes it very often. *(Oliver Herford)*

●

Women have a passion for mathematics. They divide their age in half, double the price of their clothes, and always add at least five years to the age of their friends.

(Sean Williamson)

●

It takes a woman twenty years to make a man of her son and another woman twenty minutes to make a fool of him.

(Helen Rowland)

●

In nine cases out of ten, a woman had better shown more affection than she feels. *(Jane Austen)*

●

There is no greater fan of the opposite sex than me, and I have the bills to prove it. *(Alan Jay Lerner)*

●

One needs only to see the way she is built, that woman is not intended for great mental labour.

(Arthur Schopenhauer)

Work

Work is the curse of the drinking classes.

(Osscar Wilde)

●

The brain is wonderful organ. It starts working when you get up in the morning, and does not stop until you get to the office. *(Robert Frost)*

●

They say hard work never hurt anybody, but I figure why take the chance. *(Ronald Reagan)*

●

I always arrive late at the office, but I make up for it by leaving early. *(Charles Lamb)*

●

The reason why worry kills more people than work is that more people worry than work. *(Robert Frost)*

●

The golden rule of work is that the boss' jokes are always funny. *(Robert Paul)*

●

The world is full of willing people, some willing to work, the rest willing to let them. *(Robert Frost)*

●

We have a lot of kids who don't know what works means. They think work is a four letter word. *(Hillary Clinton)*

●

People are still willing to do an honest day's work. The trouble is they want a week's pay for it.   *(Joey Adams)*

●

I like work: it fascinates me. I can sit and look at it for hours.   *(Jerome K. Jerome)*

●

If you don't want to work, you have to work to earn enough money so that you won't have to.   *(Ogden Nash)*

●

Hard work spotlights the character of people. Some turn up their sleeves, some turn up their noses, and some don't turn up at all.   *(Sam Ewing)*

●

The trouble with the rat race is that even if you win, you're still a rat.   *(Lily Tomlin)*

●

It's a shame that the only thing a man can do for eight hours is work. He can't eat for eight hours, he can't drink for eight hours, he can't make love for eight hours. The only thing a man can do for eight hours is work.

Writers

It took me fifteen years to discover that I had no talent in writing, but I couldn't give it up because by the time I was too famous.   *(Robert Benchley)*

●

There are three rules for writing a novel. Unfortunately, no one knows what they are.   *(Somerset Maugham)*

●

Asking a working writer what he thinks about critics is like asking a lamppost how it feels about dogs.

(Christopher Hampton)

●

A writer is congenitally unable to tell the truth and that is why we call his writings fiction. *(William Faulkner)*

●

American writers want to be not good but great: and so are neither. *(Gore Vidal)*

●

Our principal writers have nearly all been fortunate in escaping regular education. *(Hugh Macdiarmid)*

●

I never know what I think about something until I read what I've written on it. *(William Faulkner)*

●

Writers who stand out, as long as they are not dead, are always scandalous. *(Simon de Beauvoir)*

●

Better to write for yourself and have no public, than write for the public and have no self. *(Cyril Connolly)*

●

Talent alone cannot make a writer. There must be a man behind the book. *(Ralph Waldo Emerson)*

●

When I was a little boy they called me a liar but now that I am have grown up they call me a writer.
(Isaac Bashevis Singer)

●

Writing free verse is like playing tennis with the net down.
(Robert Frost)

●

No man but a blockhead ever wrote, except for money.
(Samuel Johnson)

●

Writing is not a profession; it is a vocation of unhappiness.
(George Simenon)

●

The profession of writing is, after all, the only one in which one can make no money without being ridiculous.

(Jules Renard)

●

Writing is like getting married. One should never commit oneself until one is amazed at one's luck.

(Iris Murdoch)

●

As long as the plots keep arriving from outer space, I'll go on with my virgins. *(Barbara Cartland)*

●

Publication is a self-invasion of privacy.
(Marshall McLuhan)

Religion

Three men of God were asked the same question: "When does life begin?"

The Catholic priest answered: "At the moment of conception."

The Anglican vicar replied "When the child is born."

And the rabbi said: "When the children are married and the mortgage has been paid off."

●

Three pastors were discussing the problems they had been experiencing with bats in their lofts.

The first said: "I introduced half a dozen cats, but the bats are still there."

The second said: "I had the place fumigated, but even that didn't work. It's still infested with bats."

The third said: "I baptised all mine and made them members of the church. I haven't seen one of them back since."

●

A priest's bicycle was stolen and he thought a member of his flock was to blame. In need of advice, he consulted his bishop who suggested that he root out the thief by preaching a sermon on the Ten Commandments. The idea was that when the priest got to "Thou shall not steal", he should pause and look around the church for anyone behaving in a guilty manner. In this way it was hoped that the culprit would give himself away.

A couple of weeks later, the bishop bumped into the priest and asked him whether the plan worked.

"Well yes," said the priest, "but not quite in the way you had envisaged. I was going through the Ten Commandments one by one, and when I got to "Thou shall not commit adultery", I remembered where I had left my bike."

●

A Sunday school teacher asked her young class: "Why is it necessary to be quiet in church?"

One boy answered: "Because people are sleeping."

●

What do you call a sleepwalking nun? A roamin' Catholic.

●

The Protestant minister met his friend, the priest and said that he dreamed about a Catholic heaven last night.

"It looked like a nice place, with plenty of pubs, bright music and people dancing about," he said.

"That's funny, said the priest. "Only last night I dreamt about a Protestant heaven. It looked nice with lots of flowerbeds, pretty trees and gardens."

"And what were the people doing?" asked the vicar.

"What people?" replied the priest.

●

There was a knock on the door and Fred found himself being asked to become a Jehovah's Witness.

Quick on his feet, Fred replied: "I didn't see the accident," and shut the door.

●

As the proud father handed the baby boy to the vicar at the christening ceremony, the cleric said: "And what will we call this little chap."

"It's a girl," whispered the father. "You've got hold of my thumb!"

●

"Father, I have sinned," said Teresa.

"What have you done my child?"

"I have committed adultery."

"How many times?"

"Just once, father"

"Well, you had better go and do it again. It's two for a dollar this week."

●

Mother Superior rapped the desk with her cane and asked the Grade IV girls what they wanted to be when they grew up.

One 13-year-old put up her hand and said: "I want to be a prostitute."

Mother Superior fainted with shock. When she was revived and had composed herself she asked the same girl: "What did you say you wanted to be?"

"A prostitute," affirmed the youngster.

"Oh, thank goodness, I thought for a moment you said you wanted to be a Protestant."

●

A drunk sat opposite a priest on the train and studied him for 10 minutes. Finally he said, "Tell me, Your Worship, why do you wear your collar back to front?"

"Because I am a father," said the priest.

"But I'm a father too," said the drunk.

"No, I am a father to hundreds in my parish."

"Then maybe it's your trousers you should be wearing back to front," said the drunk.

●

A woman was walking in the convent when one of the priests noticed she was gaining a little weight. "Gaining a little weight are we Sister Susan?" he asked.

"No Father, just a little gas."

After a month the priest noticed she had gained more weight. "Gaining some more weight are we Sister Susan?" he asked again.

"Oh no, Father, just a little gas," she replied.

A couple of months later the priest noticed Sister Susan pushing a baby carriage around the convent. He leaned over and looked in the carriage and said, "Cute little fart."

●

A priest had lost a rooster and didn't know where to find it. So at the sermon the next day he asked "Has anybody got the cock?" All the men stood up.

"No! no ! I mean has anyone seen the cock?" All the women stood up.

"No! no! I mean has anyone seen my cock?" All the nuns stood up.

●

An Englishman, a Frenchman and a Russian are viewing a painting of Adam and Eve frolicking in the Garden of Eden.

"Look at their reserve, their calm," muses the Englishman. "They must be British." "Nonsense." The Frenchman disagrees "They are naked and beautiful. Clearly they are French."

"No clothes, no shelter," the Russian points out. "They have only one apple to eat, and they are being told this is paradise. They are Russian."

●

A drunken man staggers into a Catholic Church and sits down in a confession box and says nothing. The bewildered priest coughs to attract his attention, but still the man says nothing.

The priest then knocks thrice on the wall in a final attempt to get the man to speak.

Finally the drunk replies, "No use knocking, there's no paper in this one either."

●

My wife converted me to religion. I never believed in hell until I married her.

●

A priest walked into a barber shop in Washington DC. After he got his haircut he asked how much it would be. The barber said, "No charge, I consider it a service to the Lord."

The next morning the barber came to work and there were 12 prayer books and a thank you note from the priest in front of the door.

Later that day, a police officer came in and got his hair cut. He asked how much it was. The barber said, "No charge. I consider it a service to the community."

The next morning he came to work and there were a dozen doughnuts and a thank you note from the police officer.

Then a leader came in and got a hair cut, when he was done he asked how much it was. The barber said, "No charge. I consider it a service to the country."

The next morning, the barber came to work and there were 12 leaders in front of the door.

●

A man came home from church sporting two black eyes. "What on earth happened to you?" asked his wife.

"Well, I was sitting there in church and I noticed the woman in front of me had her dress sticking in her crack. So I reached over the pew and pulled it out. And she turned round and hit me in the eye."

"All right. That explains one black eye, but what about the other one?"

"Well, I figured that must have been how she wanted her dress, so I put it back."

●

The Mother Superior was discussing the rising crime rate with one of her nuns. "Sister," she said, "what would you do if you were walking along the street at night and were accosted by a man?"

"I would raise my habit,"

The Mother Superior was shocked to hear this. "Then, what would you do?" she asked.

"I would tell him to drop his pants."

The Mother Superior was even more shocked. "And then, what would you do?"

"I would run off, because I could run faster with my habit up than he could with his pants down."

Restaurants

"Are you sure this place is hygienic?" asked the grumpy diner.

"Oh yes, Sir," replied the manager. "You could eat off the floor."

"That's the problem. It looks as if someone just has!"

●

A middle-aged man was sitting in a truck shop when three rough bikers strode in. The first walked over to the man and stubbed a cigarette into his lunch. Then the second biker spat in the man's milk. Finally the third biker picked up the man's plate of food and threw it on the floor. Without saying a word, the man got up and left.

"He wasn't much of a man, was he?" sneered one of the bikers to the waitress.

"Not much of a truck driver either," she said. "He just backed his truck over three motorcycles."

●

"Waiter! There's a fly in my soup."
"All right, I'll bring you a fork."

●

"Waiter! Your thumb's in my soup."
"That's all right, Sir. The soup's not hot."

●

"Waiter! What's this fly doing in my soup?"
"Looks like the backstroke, Sir."

●

A waiter brought a customer the steak he ordered with his thumb pressing down on the meat.

The customer was appalled. "What are you doing putting your hand on my streak?"

"Well," replied the waiter, "you wouldn't want it falling on the floor again, would you?"

●

"Waiter! What's that in my soup?"

"It's bean soup, Sir."

"I don't care what it's been. What is it now?"

●

"Waiter! This coffee tastes like mud."

"Yes Sir, it's fresh-ground."

●

"Waiter! Do you have frog's legs?"

"No Sir, it's rheumatism that makes me walk like that."

●

"Waiter! There's a dead beetle in my soup."

"Yes Sir, they're not very good swimmers."

●

"Waiter! There's fly in my soup."

"Don't worry, Sir. The spider in the bread will get it."

●

"Waiter! What's that in my soup?"

"I'd better call the manager, Sir, I can't tell one insect from another."

●

"Waiter! My plate's wet."

"It's not wet Sir; that's the soup."

●

"Waiter! What's the meaning of this fly in my soup?"

"I don't know Sir, I am a waiter not a fortune teller."

●

"Waiter! There's a dead fly in my wine."

"Well Sir, you did ask for something with a little body to it."

●

"Waiter! There's a button in my soup."

"Thank you Sir, I wondered what had happened to it."

●

"Waiter! This lobster's only got one claw."

"He must have been in a fight Sir."

"Well, bring me the winner."

●

"Waiter! There's a dead fly in my soup."

"No, Sir, that's the essential vitamin bee."

●

"Waiter! This soup is not fit for a pig."

"Very good Sir. I'll get some which is fit for a pig.

School

Physics Teacher: "Issac Newton was sitting under a tree when an apple fell on his head and he discovered gravity. Isn't that wonderful?"

Student: "Yes Sir, if he had been sitting in class looking at books like us, he wouldn't have discovered anything."

●

Teacher: "Why are you late, Joseph?"

Joseph: "Because of the sign down the road."

Teacher: "What does a sign have to do with your being late."

Joseph: "The sign said, "School Ahead, Go Slow."

●

Teacher: "In 1940, what were the Poles doing in Russia?"

Pupil: "Holding up the telegraphs lines."

●

The teacher of the earth science class was lecturing on map reading. After explaining about latitude, longitude, degrees and minutes the teacher asked, "Suppose I asked you to meet me for lunch at 23 degrees, 4 minutes north latitude and 45 degrees, 15 minutes east longitude ....?" After a confused silence, a voice volunteered,

"I guess you'd be eating alone."

●

A boy came home from his first day at school.

"So what did you learn?" asked his mother.

"Not enough. They want me to come back tomorrow," replied the boy.

●

Little John wasn't getting good marks in school. One day he surprised the teacher with an announcement. He tapped her on the shoulder and said, "I don't want to scare you, but my mother says if I don't start getting better grades, someone is going to get a spanking."

●

Teacher: "I told you to stand at the end of the line."

Pupil: "I tried, but there was someone already there."

●

Teacher: "Does anyone know which month has 28 days."

Pupil: "All of them."

●

Why was the head teacher worried?

Because there were so many rulers in the school.

●

Teacher: "Why does the Statue of Liberty stand in New York harbour?

Pupil: "Because it can't sit down."

●

A sign near the school: "Drive carefully. Don't kill the children."

A child wrote underneath: "Wait for the teacher."

●

Voice on the phone: "Johnny has a cold and can't come to school today."

School secretary: "Who is this?"

Voice: "This is my dad."

●

The teacher wrote on the blackboard:

"I ain't had no fun for months." Then she asked the class, "How should I correct the sentence?"

Little Johnny raised his hand and replied. "Get yourself a new boyfriend."

●

"I am worried about you always at the bottom of your class," said the father to his son.

"They till teach the same thing at both ends," replied the son.

●

A teacher was struggling to teach arithmetic to a young boy. So he said: "If you reached into your right pocket and found a nickel, and you reached into you left pocket and found another nickel, what would you have?"

The boy thought for a moment and replied, "Someone else's pants."

●

Teacher: "If you had one dollar and you asked your father for another dollar, how many dollars would you have?"

Boy: "One dollar."

Teacher: "You don't know your arithmetic!"

Boy: "You don't know my father."

●

Teacher: "Johnny, did your father help you with your homework last night."

Johnny: "No, he did it all."

●

Teacher: "If I bought a hundred buns for a dollar. What would each bun be?

Pupil: "Stale."

●

"Why aren't you doing well in history?" asked the mother.

"Because the teacher keeps asking about things that happened before I was born," replied the boy.

●

Teacher: "I see you missed the first day at school."

Kid: "Yes, but I didn't miss it much."

●

Teacher: "Could you please pay a little more attention."

Student: "I'm paying as little attention as I can."

●

Teacher: "You have worn your shoes on the wrong feet."

Pupil: "But these are the only feet I've got."

●

Teacher: Where's the English Channel?

Little Johnny: "I don't know, My TV doesn't pick it up."

●

Did you hear about the cross-eyed schoolteacher?

She couldn't control her pupils.

●

Ever wonder if illiterate people get the full benefit of alphabet soup?

●

A boy said to his father: "Dad, can you sign your name without looking?"

"Yes, I think so," replied the father.

"Good," said the boy. "Close you eyes and sign my school report card."

●

"Today my teacher yelled at me for something I didn't do."

"What was that?"

"My homework!"

●

A young boy arrived late at school.

"Why are you late, Johnny?" asked the teacher.

"I am sorry, Miss, but I had to get my own breakfast today."

"All right, Johnny," said the teacher, "never mind. Now today we are doing geography and here is a map of the British Isles. Can anyone tell me where the Scottish border is?"

"Yes Miss," said Johnny, "in bed with my mum. That's why I had to get my own breakfast."

●

A schoolteacher asked her class what their parents did for a living. Little Johnny put up his hand and said: "My mum is a substitute."

Knowing something of the family background, the teacher said: "I think you mean she's a prostitute."

"No," said Johnny. "My big sister is the prostitute but when she doesn't feel well, Mum acts as a substitute."

●

A history teacher was taking a lesson on the kings and queens of England. "Do you know who followed Edward VI?" she asked.

"Mary," replied a boy at the back.

"That's right," said the teacher. "And who followed Mary?"

"Her little lamb," said the boy.

●

Teacher: "It's clear that you haven't studied your geography. What is your excuse?"

Pupil: "Well, my dad says the world is changing every day, so I decided to wait till it settles down."

●

Teacher: "What do you want to be when you grow up?"

Little Johnny: "I want to follow in my father's footsteps and be a policeman."

Teacher: "I didn't know your father was a policeman."

Little Johnny: "He isn't. He's a burglar!"

Signs

In a health shop window: Closed due to illness.

●

In a barber shop: Haircutting while you wait.

●

On a plumber's van: We repair what your husband fixed.

●

In a shop window: We exchange everything – bicycles, washing machines, etc. Bring your wife and get the deal of your life.

●

In a restaurant window: Don't stand there and be hungry. Come on in and get fed up.

●

Laundry: Ladies please leave your cloths here and spend the afternoon having good fun.

●

Hotel: The manager has personally passed all the water served here.

●

Petrol Station: Please do not smoke near our petrol pumps. Your life may not be worth much, but our petrol is.

●

Zoo: Please do not feed the animals. If you have any suitable food, give it to the guard on duty.

●

In an office: Would the person who took the step ladder yesterday, please bring it back or further steps will be taken.

●

On the church door: This is the gate of heaven. This door is kept locked because of draughts.

●

Pizza shop slogan: Seven days without pizza makes one weak.

●

In a tailor's shop: Customers giving orders will be promptly executed.

●

In a hotel: Ladies are requested not to have children in the Cocktail Room.

●

In a restaurant: Steaks and chops are grilled before our customers.

●

On a church notice board: Don't let worries kill you. Let the church help.

●

In a supermarket: For your convenience, we recommend courageous, efficient self-service.

●

On the door of a maternity ward: Push, push, push.

●

In a department store: Bargain basement upstairs.

●

Outside the pub: Beer cheaper than petrol. Drink, don't drive.

●

In a beauty shop: Dye now.

●

In a maternity hospital: Visitors – Husbands only; one per patient.

●

At a railway station: Toilets out of order, please use platforms 7-8.

●

Outside a funeral parlour: Parking for clients only.

●

Near a donkey ride: Would you like to ride on your own ass?

●

In a tourist agency: Take one of our horse-driven city tours...we guarantee no miscarriages.

●

In an optician's shop: If you don't see what you're looking for, you've come to the right place.

●

In a pub: If you are drinking to forget, please pay for your drinks in advance.

●

In a shop window: Out to lunch. If not back by five, out to dinner also.

●

In a restaurant window: Try our home-made pies. You will never get better.

●

Outside a factory: Closing down, thanks to all our customers.

●

Outside a disco: Members and non-members only.

●

In a shop window: Model willing to pose for a nude artist.

●

On the door of a Moscow hotel room: If this is your first visit to the USSR, you are welcome to it.

●

On a plumber's van: Don't sleep with your drip, call your plumber.

●

Outside a tailor's shop: Ladies may have a fit upstairs.

●

In a jeweller's shop: Our gifts will not last long at these prices.

●

In a hotel bathroom: Instant hot water, in two minutes.

●

In a shop: Prices subject to change, according to the customer's attitude.

●

Sign on an electric transmitter's big box: To touch these wires means instant death. Anyone doing so will be prosecuted.

●

Sign on Butcher's Shop: Try our tongues. They speak for themselves.

Our sausages are fit for the Queen.

Sign on shop opposite: God save the Queen.

Smart Rejections

Hi, gorgeous. Where have you been all my life?

Well, for most of it I wasn't born.

●

Your body is like a temple. Sorry, there are no services today.

●

If I could see you naked, I'd die happy. If I could see you naked, I'd die laughing.

●

Hey, baby, what is your sign? Do not enter.

●

Your place or mine? Both. You go to your place, and I'll go to mine.

●

I'd really like to get into your pants. No thanks, there is already one asshole in there.

●

Haven't we met before? Yes, I'm a receptionist at the VD clinic.

●

I'd go through anything for you. Let's start with your bank account.

●

Hi, sexy, fancy a drink? I like your approach. Now let's see your departure.

●

If you come home with me, I can show you a real good time.
You know your problem? Your mouth is writing cheques that your body can't cash.

●

Is this seat empty? Yes, and this one will be too if you sit down.

●

When can I take you out? How about never. Is never good for you?

●

I would go to the end of the world for you. Yes, but would you stay there?

●

What's a nice girl like you doing in a place like that? What's a nice guy like you doing with a face like that?

●

So how about a date? I am busy now. Can I ignore you some other time?

●

I can tell that you want me. Yes, I want you to leave.

●

What are your sexual preferences? My sexual preference is "No".

●

I know how to please a woman. Then please leave me alone.

●

Haven't I seen you some place before? Yes, that's why I don't go there any more.

●

Do you mind if I sit here?

Sorry, I can't talk to you right now. Tell me, where you will be in ten years.

Time

A tourist visiting an archaeological site in South America was intrigued by the display of dinosaur bones. She asked a local Indian, who was acting as a tourist guide, how old the bones were.

"Exactly 100 million and three years old," replied the Indian.

"That's amazing," said the tourist. "How can you be so precise?"

"Simple," said the Indian. "A geologist told me they were 100 million years old, and that was exactly three years ago."

•

After driving all night, a company rep was still a log way from home as dawn broke. He decided to pull over and catch up on his sleep for a couple of hours. Unknown to him, he had chosen to park his car on the city's main jogging route. Barely had he dozed off then he was startled by a knock on the car window. It was a jogger.

"What's the time?" asked the jogger.

"Seven fifteen," said the man drowsily. He tried to doze but soon another jogger knocked on his window.

"What's the time?" yelled the jogger.

"Seven thirty," said the man, irritated. Again, he tried to get to sleep, but was quickly awakened by another jogger hammering on the window.

"What's the time?" he screamed.

"Seven forty-five." snapped the man. That was the last straw. Taking a pen and paper, he put a sign in his car window saying, "I do not know the time!"

No sooner had he fallen asleep again when another jogger was pounding on the window, shouting: "Hey, buddy.. It's seven fifty-five."

●

A man arrived at a small county station ready to catch the 8:30 train. Spotting that the clock outside the station said 8:25, he thought he had enough time to buy a newspaper. But after hurriedly purchasing his paper, he stepped on the platform just as his train was disappearing into the distance. He looked up at the platform clock and saw that it said 8:35. When he protested to the station master about the discrepancy between the two clocks, the station master replied, "Well, why would we need two clocks if they both told the same time?"

●

A smooth-talking guy at a bar kept looking at his watch. An attractive woman couldn't help noticing this and asked: "Is your date late?"

"No," he said. "I just bought this state-of-the-art watch and I was testing it. It uses alpha waves to talk to me."

"What's it telling you?"

"That you're not wearing any panties."

"Well, sorry," she said, "but I am."

"Damn, it must be an hour late."

●

While proudly showing off his new apartment to friends, a college student led the way into the den.

"What is the big brass gong and hammer for?" one of his friends asked.

"That is a talking clock," the man replied.

"How does it work?" the friend asked.

"Watch," the man said and then proceeded to give the gong an ear shattering pound with the hammer.

Suddenly someone screamed from the other side of the wall.

"KNOCK IT OFF, YOU IDIOT! It's 2 a.m. in the morning."

●

Even though he could not tell the time, my three-year-old grandson was wearing a watch when I visited. Later, when I was putting on my coat to leave, I asked him what time it was. He looked at his watch blankly, then brightened.

"It's time for you to go," he answered triumphantly.

●

A social worker asks his mate: "What time is it?"

The mate answers: "Sorry, I don't know, I don't have a watch."

The social worker said, "Never mind! The main thing is that we talked about it."

●

We spend our lives on the run. We get up by the clock, eat and sleep by the clock, get up again, go to work. And then we retire. And what do they give us?

A bloody clock!

●

What dog can tell the time? A watchdog.

●

What time is it when an elephant sits in your car? Time to get a new car.

●

When do clocks die? When their time is up.

●

What is the best time to go shopping? When the stores are open.

●

Why couldn't the clock be kept in jail? Because time was always running out.

●

Why is the time in the US behind that of England? Because England was discovered before the US.

●

Why do people beat the clock? To kill time.

The USA

Bill, Hillary and George Bush die and are brought before God. God looks at Bush and asks, "Who are you?"

He says "I am George Bush, President of the USA."

God thinks, nods his head and says, "Then you can sit on the chair to my right."

God then looks at Bill Clinton and asks, "Who are you?"

Bill says, "I am Bill Clinton, former President of the USA."

God nods his head and says, "Then you can sit on the chair to my left."

God then looks at Hillary and asks, "Who are you?"

Hillary replies, "I am Hillary Clinton, and I believe you are in my seat."

●

On a train from London to Manchester, an American was telling off an Englishman sitting across from him in the compartment.

"You English are too stuffy. You set yourself apart too much. Look at me.... I have Italian blood, French blood, a little Indian blood, and some Swedish blood. What do you say to that?"

The Englishman replied with smile. "Very sporting of your mother."

●

An avid Canadian fisherman decides to cross the Peace Bridge and go over to Lewiston to fish on the American side of the Niagara river. He settles down with some nice fish when an American warden approaches him and says, "Could I see your fishing licence please?"

When he hands him his licence, the game warden laughs and says that it is no good because it is a Canadian fishing licence. At this point the fisherman replies, "But I am catching Canadian fish." The warden scratches his head for a moment and says "What do you mean?"

The fisherman reaches into his bucket and pulls out a fish and asks the warden. "What kind of fish is that?" The warden looks at it and says, "It's a small mouth bass," to which the fisherman replies, "See what I mean, if it was an American fish it would be a large mouth bass."

●

An American girl was visiting England and was invited to a party. While dancing with an Englishman, her necklace became unfastened and slipped down the back of her dress.

She asked the Englishman to retrieve the jewellery for her.

He was very embarrassed but wishing to comply with her request he reached cautiously down the back of her gown.

"I am terribly sorry, but I can't seem to reach it." he said.

"Try further down," she said.

At this point he noticed that he was being watched by everyone in the room which made him feel uncomfortable and he whispered to the girl, "I feel such a perfect ass."

"Thanks," she said, "But never mind that! Just get the necklace."

●

One Sunday in January 2009 an old man approached the White Hose. He spoke to the US Marine standing guard and said, "I would like to go in and meet President Bush.

The Marine looked at the man and said, "Sir, Mr. Bush is no longer the President and does not reside here."

The old man said, "All right," and walked away.

The following day the same man approached the White House and said to the same Marine, "I would like to go in and meet President Bush."

The Marine told the man, "Sir, I told you yesterday, Mr. Bush is no longer the President and does not reside here."

The man thanked him again and just walked away.

On the third day the man approached the White House and spoke to the very same Marine saying, "I would like to go in and meet President Bush."

The Marine was understandably agitated at this point. He looked at the man and said, "Sir, this is the third day in a row you have come here asking to meet Mr. Bush. I have told you already that Mr. Bush is no longer the President and does not reside here. Don't you understand?"

The old man looked at the Marine and said, "Oh I understand, I just love to hear it."

The Marine snapped to attention, saluted, and said, "See you tomorrow Sir."

●

A Washington DC airport ticket agent offers some examples of why the US. is in trouble:

A Mexico woman called to make reservation, "I want to go from Chicago to Rhino, New York." I was at a loss for words. Finally, I said, "Are you sure that's the name of the town?"

"Yes, what flight do you have?" replied the lady.

After some searching, I came back with, "I am sorry, ma'am, I have looked up every airport code in the country and I can't find Rhino anywhere."

The lady retorted, "Oh, don't be silly! Everyone knows where it is. Check your map."

So I scoured a map of the state of New York and finally offered, "You don't mean Buffalo, do you?" The reply was. "Whatever! I know it was a big animal."

●

I just got off the phone with a Congresswoman who asked "How do I know which plane to get on?"
I asked her what exactly she meant, to which she replied "I was told my flight number is 823, but none of these planes have numbers on them."

●

An Illinois American called up last week. He wanted to know how it was possible for his flight to take off from Detroit at 8.30 am. and land at Chicago at 8.33 am. I explained that Michigan was an hour ahead of Illinois, but he couldn't understand the concept of time zones. Finally, I told him the plane was very fast and he bought the ticket.

●

I had a New York congresswoman ask for an aisle seat so that her hair wouldn't get messed up by being near the window.

●

If a person who speaks three languages is called "tri-lingual" and a person who speaks two languages is called "bi-lingual", what do you call a person who speaks one language?
"American."

●

An American journalist once asked Mahatma Gandhi, "What is your opinion about civilisation?"
Gandhi smiled and replied, "I think it would be an excellent idea."

●

What is the difference between Americans and bacteria?
If you leave bacteria on their own for 20 years they are more likely to develop   culture.....

●

It is terrible the way people keep making jokes about obese Americans.

I mean, haven't they got enough on their plates?

●

Only In the US:
Do people order double cheeseburgers, large fries and a diet coke.

●

Do banks leave their doors open and chain the pens to the counters.

●

Do people leave cars worth thousands of dollars in the driveway and put useless junk in the garage.

●

Do people buy hot dogs in packets of ten and buns in the packets of eight.

●

Is a man who invests all your money called a broker.

●

Are houses called apartments when they are all stacked together.

●

Telltale signs that you're from the US
❑ You believe that being able to swear at people in their own language makes you multilingual.
❑ You go to a hockey game for fighting.
❑ Your door has more than three locks.
❑ The most frequently used part of your car is the horn.
❑ You've never been to the Statue of Liberty or the Empire Building.
❑ You consider eye contact to be an overt act of aggression.
❑ You get arthritis in your middle finger from over-use.
❑ The subway makes sense.

Women

If your dog is barking at the back door and your wife is yelling at the front door, who do you let it first?

The dog. At least he'll shut up after you let him in.

●

In the beginning, God created earth and rested. Then God created man and rested. Then God created woman. Since then, neither God nor man has rested.

●

A woman said to her friend: "I made my husband a millionaire."

And what was he before you married him?"

"A billionaire."

●

When does a woman enjoy a man's company? When he owns it.

●

Why did God make man first? He didn't want a woman looking over his shoulder.

●

The signs indicate that women really are far lazier than men. You see lots of places marked "Men's Toilets" but you see even more places marked "Ladies' Rest Room".

●

At a women's wear trade show, a buyer approached a booth where a bra manufacturer had displayed his bras.

"Anything new in bras this year?"

"No," was the answer. "Women are wearing the same thing in bras this year as they were last year."

●

At various times in her life, a woman is like the continents of the world. From 13 to 18, she is like Africa – virgin territory: from 18 to 30, like Asia – hot and exotic: from 30 to 45, she's like Europe – exhausted, but not without places of interest: from 55 onwards, she's like Australia – everyone knows it's down there, but nobody cares.

●

With the plane about to plunge into a mountain, a female passenger stood up and shouted: "If I'm going to die, I want to die feeling like a woman."

She took off her top and cried: "Is there someone on this plane who is man enough to make me feel like a woman?"

Hearing this, a man stood up, took off his shirt and said: "Iron this."

●

A woman is the only hunter that uses herself for bait.

●

Woman to a shop assistant: "I need a size 30 bra."
Shop assistant: "What size cup?"
Woman: "I should say saucer."

●

What are women's favourite animals?
A mink in the closet; a jaguar in the garage; a tiger in the bedroom; and an ass to pay for it all.

●

Why are married women heavier than single women?
Single women come home, see what is in the refrigerator and go to bed.
Married women come home, see what's in the bed and go to the refrigerator.

●

What is the difference between a battery and a woman?
A battery has a positive side.

●

Would a clever woman make a good wife? A clever woman wouldn't become a wife.

●

Why do women have smaller feet than men? So that they can stand closer to the sink.

●

Why does a woman close her eyes during sex?
Because no woman ever wants to see a man enjoying himself.

●

A woman walked into a drugstore and asked the pharmacist if he sold extra large condoms?
"Yes, we do. Would you like to buy some?"
"No, but do you mind if I wait here till someone does?"

●

What's six inches long, two inches wide and drives women wild? Money.

●

Women are incomplete without men. Take away 'men' from women and all that remains is 'woe'.

●

John: "Did you ever see a group of women that was silent?"
Tom: "Yes."
John: "When?"
Tom: "When the chairman asked the oldest woman to speak."

●

A woman in need is a woman indeed.

●

Zoos

A kangaroo kept escaping from his enclosure at the zoo. Knowing how high he could hop, the keepers erected a new ten-foot-high fence, but the following morning the kangaroo had got out again. So they put up a 20-foot fence, but still the kangaroo managed to escape.

Watching all this, the llama in the next enclosure said: "How high do you think they'll go?"

The kangaroo replied: "It doesn't matter unless someone remembers to lock the gate at night."

●

A baby camel turned to his father and said: "Dad, why we do have humps on our back?"

"Well son," replied the father, "our humps contain fat necessary to sustain us through all the days when we're out in the desert."

"Oh," said the baby camel. "Dad why do we have long eyelashes?"

They're to protect our eyes from the sandstorms which rage in the desert."

"Fine, Dad, why do we have big padded feet?"

"Because the sand in the desert is very soft and we need big feet so that we can walk on the sand without sinking."

"Thanks, Dad. So what are we doing in the London Zoo?"

●

Needing a star attraction for the summer, a cash-strapped zoo persuaded a visitor to dress up in a gorilla costume and pretend to be a great ape. The ruse worked well as the man threw himself into the role with great enthusiasm, devouring bucket loads of bananas, prowling his cage with menace and banging his chest dramatically. But then one day, he went too far and accidentally fell into the lion's cage next door.

"Help! Help!" cried the gorilla.

The lion let out an almighty roar, then rushed at him, put his paw on his chest and growled: "Shut up, or we'll both lose our jobs."

●

A police officer saw a truck being driven erratically. On closer inspection, he noticed that there were 140 penguins in the back of the truck and pulled the driver over for unlawful possession of animals. But when the driver explained that he was taking the penguins to the zoo, the officer relented.

"All right, I'll let you off this time, as long as you are definitely taking them to the zoo."

The following day, the officer saw the same truck weaving along the road, and once again there were 140 penguins in the back of the truck. He stopped the truck and said to the driver: "I thought you told me yesterday you were taking the penguins to the zoo."

"I was," said the driver. "And today I'm taking them to a theme park."

●

A father and his small son were standing in front of the tiger's cage at the zoo.

The father was explaining how ferocious and strong tigers are and junior was taking it all in with a serious expression.

"Dad", the boy said finally, "if the tiger got out of his cage and ate you up...."

"Yes, son," the father said expectantly.

"What bus should I take home?" the boy finished.

●

Two middle-aged spinsters, Kay and Liz, went to the zoo one afternoon. When they reached the gorilla's enclosure, the gorilla suddenly pulled Liz into his den and molested her.

A few weeks later, the two women met in the street. Kay asked Liz how she was doing after the attack.

"Well, how do you think?" snapped Liz. "He hasn't called, he hasn't written."

●

One day the zookeeper noticed that the ape was reading two books – the Bible and Darwin's *Origin of Species*. In surprise he asked the ape, "Why are you reading both these books?"

Well," said the ape, "I just wanted to know if I was my brother's keeper or my keeper's brother."

●

Fred's class was taken to the Natural History Museum in New York.

"Did you enjoy yourself?" asked his mother when he got home.

"Oh yes," replied Fred. "But it was funny going to a dead zoo."

●

A man went to work for a zoo veterinarian. "Look into the lion's mouth," the vet told him.

"How do I do that?" he asked.

"Carefully," replied the vet.

●

My wife asked me to take her to the zoo the other day. I said, "If you want people to see you, they can come here and do so."

●

In the United States, what is the difference between a northern zoo and a southern zoo?"

In a northern zoo, you have the name of the animal and the Latin name below. In a southern zoo, you have the name of the animal and a recipe underneath.

●

Zoo keeper: "I've lost my elephant."

Other zoo keeper: "Why don't you put an advert in the paper?"

Zoo keeper: "Don't be silly, he can't read."

●

Q. Why did the Irishman buy two tickets to go to the zoo?

A. One to get in and one to get out.

●

A man told his friend that he was at the zoo last week. The friend asked, "Which cage were you in?"

●

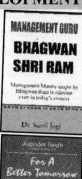

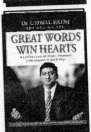

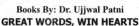

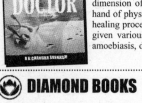